JEWELRY
HANDBOOK
How to Select, Wear & Care for Jewelry

Above: An array of jewelry from Hubert Inc., which includes a pearl necklace and earr[ings]
and rings set with aquamarine, sapphire, green tourmaline, yellow sapphire and diamo[nds].
Photo by GNG Photography.

Opposite page: Rings by Zaffiro set with pink sapphire, freshwater pearl, spessartite ga[rnet],
opalized petrified wood, turquoise, rose quartz, green tourmaline, purple sapphire,
chalcedony and pink tourmaline. 22K gold, 18K gold and platinum were used fo[r]
mountings and granulation. *Photo by Daniel Van Rossen.*

JEWELRY
HANDBOOK
How to Select, Wear & Care for Jewelry

Renée Newman

International Jewelry Publications
Los Angeles

391.7
NEW

This publication is designed to provide information in
regard to the subject matter covered. It is sold with the un-
derstanding that the publisher and author are not engaged in
rendering legal, financial, or other professional services. If
legal or other expert assistance is required, the services of a
competent professional should be sought. International Jewelry
Publications and the author shall have neither liability nor
responsibility to any person or entity with respect to any loss
or damage caused or alleged to be caused directly or indirectly
by the information contained in this book. All inquiries should
be directed to:

International Jewelry Publications
P.O. Box 13384
Los Angeles, CA 90013-0384 USA

(Inquiries should be accompanied by a self-addressed, stamped
envelope.)

Printed in Singapore

Library of Congress Cataloging-in-Publication Data

Newman, Renée.
  Jewelry handbook : How to select, wear & care for jewelry /
Renée Newman.
    p. cm.
  Includes bibliographical references and index.
  ISBN-13: 978-0-929975-38-2 (paper)
1. Jewelry–Purchasing. I. Title.
  TS729.N484 2007
  391.7–de22
                          2006049645

Cover photo:
An array of jewelry created by Paula Crevoshay:
A double strand necklace of apatite faceted beads
A 5.22-carat black opal ring complimented by diamonds and
Paraiba tourmalines
A 28.72-carat smithsonite ring accented by moonstones
A 10.06 carat opal ring accented by diamonds and tourmalines
A pair of black opal earrings complimented by Namibian
demantoid garnets, Paraiba tourmalines, and diamonds
Photo copyright 2004 by Azad

Contents

1. Why Wear Jewelry? 1

What This Book is Not   4

What This Book is   6

2. Jewelry Metals: Key Facts   7

Terms Related to Gold and Platinum Content   7

Platinum Content and Notation   9

Terms Related to Metals and Imitation Gold   10

Weights, Measures, and Marks   14

Miscellaneous Terms   16

Which is Better: 14K or 18K Gold?   17

Silver Jewelry   18

Other White Metals Used for Jewelry   21

  Palladium   21

  Titanium   24

  Stainless Steel   26

  Tungsten   26

3. Basic Facts about Gems   29

Gemstone Terms Defined   29

Traditional Cutting Styles   31

Non-traditional Cuts   39

Birthstones and Anniversary Stones   42

4. Manufacturing Methods   45

Lost Wax Casting   45

Stamping (Die Striking)   49

Electroforming   51

Hand Fabrication   52

Handmade Jewelry 54

Why Manufacturing Methods are Often Combined   55

5. **Selecting the Setting   57**
    Choosing a Secure Prong (Claw) Setting   57
    Other Setting Styles   60
        Bezel setting   60
        Channel setting   62
        Bead or pavé Setting   64
        Flush setting   65
        Invisible setting   66

6. **Finishes & Decorative Techniques   67**
    Finishes   67
    Decorative Techniques   69
    Judging the Finish   77

7. **Choosing Flattering Jewelry   79**

8. **Selecting Necklaces   83**
    Necklace Lengths and Styles   83
    Selecting Flattering Necklaces   87

9. **Chains and Other Neckwear   91**
    Chain Lengths   92
    Advantages and Drawbacks of Various Chains   92
    Other Neckwear Options   100
    Tips on Selecting Clasps   103

10. **Selecting Rings   109**
    Selecting a Flattering Ring   110
    Practical Tips on Selecting Rings   110
    Selecting a Ring Size   115

11. **Selecting Earrings   121**
    Earring Types and Styles   121
    Selecting Flattering Earrings   124

12. **Selecting Bracelets   127**
    Bracelet Types   128
    Tips on Selecting Bracelets   128

13. **Brooches, Pins and Clips   133**

Contents

14. Making Jewelry Versatile   139

15. Jewelry Tips for Men   149

16. Caring for Your Jewelry   153
Cleaning Metal Mountings   154
Cleaning Gemstones   157
Cleaning Pearls   160
Miscellaneous Tips   161

Suppliers of the Jewelry for Photos in This Book   163

Bibliography   169

Index   173

Acknowledgments

I would like to express my appreciation to the following people and companies for their contribution to the *Jewelry Handbook*:

Ernie and Regina Goldberger of the Josam Diamond Trading Corporation. This book could never have been written without the experience and knowledge I gained from working with them.

Debra Sawatsky and Miranda Hayes Schultz who inspired and encouraged me to write this book.

Eve Alfillé, Paul Cassarino, Mark Castagnoli, Elaine Ferrari Santhon, Scott Hallock, Miranda Hayes Schulz, Jurgen Maerz, Karen McGinn, Mark B. Mann, Patara Marlow, Steve Mikaelian, Elise Misiorowski. Corrine Perez-Garcia, Debra Petres, Alan Revere, Debra Sawatsky, Sindi Schloss, Kathrin Schoenke, and Dale Swanson. They've made valuable suggestions, corrections and comments regarding the portions of the book they examined. They're not responsible for any possible errors, nor do they necessarily endorse the material contained in this book.

A & A Findings, Aaron Henry, Aurora Imports Inc., Benjamin & Co., Peggy Croft, Mark Fischer, Gelin & Abaci, Hallock Jewelry, Inc., Josam Diamond Trading Corp, Jane Keller, Kevorks Jewelry, LRG Studio 13, Inc., Garbis Mazmanian, Media Imports, Inc., Gregory Mikaelian & Sons Inc., Jane Nordvedt, Judy Pack, Pure Gold, Alan Revere, Varna Platinum, Sandra Weaver and Nerses Yahiayan. Jewelry, chains, and/or related materials from them were loaned for some of the photographs.

A & A Jewelry Supplies, A & Z Pearls, Aaron Henry Designs, Abe Mor Diamond Cutters & Co., Alan Hodgkinson, Alan Revere, Angela Conty, Art Carved, Aurora Imports, Barbara Westwood, Bobby Mann, Carolyn Tyler, Christian Tse, Dancing Designs, Divina Pearls, Eve J. Alfillé, FDJ On Time LLC, Forest Jewelers, Fred & Kate Pearce, Gary Dulac Goldsmith,

Acknowledgments

Gemological Institute of America, George Sawyer, Grobet USA, H. S. Walsh & Sons Ltd, Heavy Stone Rings, HOOKer Earrings, Hubert Inc, J. Landau, Inc., Jemco Jewelry Supply, JFF Jewelry Supply, John Dyer, Joseph DuMouchelle Auctioneers, K. Brunini Jewels, Karen R. McGinn, King Plutarco, Inc, LRG Studio, Mahlia Collection, Mark Schneider, Media Imports, Oliver & Espig Jewelers, Palladium Alliance International (PAI), Paula Crevoshay, Rubin & Son, Sajen, Inc., Sherris Cottier Shank, Stamper Black Hills Gold Jewelry, Stuller, Inc., Sugarman-Frantz Designs, Sweet Iron Silver Co.,Tempus Gems, The Bell Group, ,The Roxx Limited, Timeless Gem Designs, Todd Reed, True Knots, Varna, Winc Creations, Zaffiro, and Zava Master Cuts. Photos or diagrams from them have been reproduced in this book.

Bonnie Nelson, Don Nelson and Joyce Ng. They have provided technical assistance.

Louise Harris Berlin. She has spent hours carefully editing the *Jewelry Handbook*. Thanks to her, this book is much easier for consumers to read and understand.

My sincere thanks to all of these contributors for their kindness and help.

1

Why Wear Jewelry?

According to the Latin and French derivation, "jewelry" means joy. Throughout history, a prime reason for wearing jewelry was to add a dimension of happiness and excitement to life. Prehistoric man wanted more than just food, shelter and clothing, so he created jewelry from materials such as bone, teeth, rocks, shells, hair and feathers. Later, materials such as clay, glass, precious metals and gemstones were used.

Jewelry has served many functions. These include:

♦ Personal adornment

♦ Expressions of love, affection and commitment

♦ Good luck charms and talismans with magical powers

♦ Portable storage of wealth and hedge against inflation

♦ Religious symbols

♦ Artistic expressions of beauty

♦ Ideal gifts and remembrances for special occasions

♦ Useful purposes such as belt buckles, buttons, pins, cufflinks, watches, signets, medical ID bracelets, rings with secret departments filled with perfume, disinfectant or messages.

♦ Healing aids. The therapeutic use of gems and jewelry is growing.

♦ Political statements. For example, around 1900, women who wanted the right to vote wore pins and pendants featuring green, white and violet stones. These were the suffragette colors with their initials standing for "Give Women the Vote."

Unconventional, Yet Traditional Jewelry Materials

Fig. 1.1 African batiked mud beads. *Bracelet and photo from Sajen™.*

Fig. 1.2 A brooch made from human hair. It was created and photographed by Karen McGinn, a jeweler, artist, designer and appraiser. Pieces made from the hair of family members are unique, sentimental gifts.

Fig. 1.3 Coconut wood drops set in 22K gold over sterling (vermeil). *Earrings and photo from Sajen™.*

Fig. 1.4 Bone pendant probably carved from a cow bone. *Photo by bone and ivory identification specialist Bobby Mann.*

Jewelry is commonly divided into two categories:

Fine jewelry A term for jewelry made with gold, platinum or palladium and often set with gemstones. It probably originates from the expression "fine gold," which is gold in its purest form. Like gold and the platinum group of metals, silver is classified as a precious metal and can also be considered a component of fine jewelry. However, because of its significantly lower cost, some trade members prefer to classify it as a transitional metal which can either be used for fine jewelry or fashion jewelry.

Costume jewelry Twentieth century term for jewelry that is plated or not made of gold or metals from the platinum group. Costume jewelry often contains synthetic or imitation gems, but it may also be set with real gemstones such as blue topaz, agate and black onyx. Sometimes costume jewelry is called **fashion jewelry**.

There are **subcategories** of fine and costume jewelry which include:

Designer jewelry Created by a jewelry designer, and usually bearing the name, signature or identifying pattern of the designer.

Custom jewelry Individually made to order. Often one-of-a-kind.

Antique jewelry One-hundred or more years old, as defined by the U.S. Customs Bureau. Webster's dictionary defines the term "antique" more loosely—any work of art or the like from an early period.

Estate jewelry Previously owned by someone and typically passed on from one generation to another. It can range from a few decades to 100 or more years in age. It may also be called **heirloom jewelry** or **vintage jewelry**.

Collectible jewelry	Gathered from a specific designer, manufacturer, or any period or periods in time. The pieces are collected according to the buyer's interests, and normally they are no longer in production, but they don't have to be as old as antiques. For example, retro jewelry pieces are considered collectibles, but they are not true antiques. Hence the phrase, "antiques and collectibles."
Body jewelry	Usually refers to jewelry worn in the nose, lips, belly, navel, tongue, eyebrow, nipples or on the toes—not in the ears, or on the fingers, wrists and neck. Piercing is required for most body jewelry. Nose piercing was first recorded in the Middle East about four thousand years ago. Navel piercing, on the other hand, is a relatively new form of body jewelry that originated after the invention of the bikini in 1953.
Artisan jewelry	Handcrafted from a variety of materials including various types of wire, wood, hair, plastic, bone, fabric, vinyl, paper, clay, shell, rubber and Plexiglass. It's also called **craft jewelry**.

Jewelry can overlap into more than one category. Some artisan jewelry can be considered designer jewelry. And from the standpoint of price and craftsmanship, some costume jewelry qualifies as fine jewelry. It's not uncommon nowadays for designers to mount synthetic gems or low-priced gems in gold. Similarly, expensive gems are sometimes mounted in titanium or stainless steel.

This book focuses more on fine jewelry than costume jewelry, but the principles and information that are discussed are applicable to all types of jewelry.

What This Book Is Not

♦ This book is not a guide to making, repairing, or designing jewelry. Many helpful books have been written on these subjects; some are listed in the bibliography.

Fig. 1.5 Cocobollo wood cuffs by K. Brunini Jewels. *Photo by Chris Trayer.*

Fig. 1.6 Fossilized coral, red jasper face, pink shell heart and rose quartz flower. *Pin/pendant and photo from Sajen™.*

Fig. 1.7 African mud bead set in silver. *Pendant and photo from Sajen™.*

Fig. 1.8 Abalone shell stretch bracelet. *Jewelry and photo from Sajen™.*

♦ This book is not a catalog of jewelry styles. Those can be obtained at jewelry stores and on the Internet.

♦ This book is not a price guide. Metal prices can change daily, and jewelry prices are determined by a variety of factors—quality of the craftsmanship, complexity of the design, the mode of manufacture, the geographic area where the jewelry is produced, etc. However, a knowledge of the principles discussed in this book will help you compare prices more accurately.

What This Book Is

♦ A visual guide to selecting jewelry that enhances your appearance and suits your lifestyle and budget

♦ A handy reference on jewelry terminology and concepts

♦ A collection of practical tips on wearing and caring for jewelry

♦ An aid to avoiding disappointments with jewelry that does not last or fit your needs

♦ A source of creative jewelry ideas for lay people and professionals

Shopping for jewelry should not be a chore; it should be fun. The more you know about jewelry, the more you'll appreciate it and enjoy it. Use this book to gain the knowledge and confidence needed to select the jewelry that's best for you. Buying jewelry represents a significant investment of time and money. Let the *Jewelry Handbook* help make this investment a pleasurable and rewarding experience.

2

Jewelry Metals: Key Facts

Copper was probably the first jewelry metal. It's malleable, resilient and attractive, but it not only discolors when worn, it also discolors the skin, typically by turning it green. Nevertheless, copper is still an important metal in the production of silver and gold jewelry alloys.

The second jewelry metal was probably gold. Because of its luster, rarity, malleability and resistance to corrosion, it has always been highly valued. However, in some ancient cultures, silver was more valued than gold because it was harder to find.

Values and preferences change with time. Recently, in many parts of the world, platinum has been the preferred metal for top quality bridal jewelry. However, with the increasing cost of platinum, many buyers looking for white metal rings are choosing white gold or palladium, another platinum group metal.

When selecting jewelry, you should consider the type of metal used because it affects the value, durability, and requirements for care. Jewelry metals are seldom pure. This chapter explains the terminology used to describe metal content, weights, measures and marks, and it gives practical information about the various jewelry metals in order to help you make wise selections.

Terms Related to Gold & Platinum Content

Alloy   A mixture of two or more metals made by melting them together. Gold, for example, is alloyed (combined) with metals such as silver, copper, zinc and nickel to reduce its cost and change characteristics such as its color and hardness. **Platinum alloys** are usually made by combining platinum with ruthenium, palladium, cobalt, iridium or copper.

Fine gold   Gold containing no other elements or metals. It's also called pure gold or 24K (24 karat) gold and has a fineness of 999.

Fineness   The amount of gold or platinum in relation to 1000 parts. For example, gold with a fineness of 750 has 750 parts (75%) gold and 250 parts of other metals. An alloy containing 95% platinum and 5% ruthenium has a fineness of 950.

Karat (Carat) A measure of gold purity. One karat is 1/24 pure, so 24 karat is pure gold. Do not confuse "karat," the unit of gold purity, with "carat," the unit of weight for gemstones. These two words originate from the same source, the Italian *carato* and the Greek *karation* which mean "fruit of the carob tree." In ancient times, carob beans were used as counterweights when weighing gems and gold. Outside the US, "karat" is often spelled "carat," particularly in countries which are members of the British Commonwealth.

Karat gold   A gold alloy, which in the United States must have a fineness of at least 10K. In Britain, Spain, Japan and Canada, it must be at least 9K and in Mexico and Germany 8K. Gold must be at least 18K in France and Italy to be called gold. For detailed information on US government gold and jewelry terminology regulations see http://www.ftc.gov/bcp/guides/jewel-gd.htm.

Plumb gold   In general usage, it means gold that has the same purity
(KP)   as the mark stamped on it. Therefore, 14KP means gold that is really 14K. Prior to 1978 in the US, 13K gold jewelry which had been soldered could be stamped 14K. According to current US and Canadian law, the pure gold content must be within 3 parts per thousand of the stamped karat mark for unsoldered items and 7 parts per thousand for soldered items. When jewelers describe their jewelry as plumb gold, they are emphasizing that they abide by the law because not all jewelers do.

Pure gold   Same as fine gold

Solid gold   Gold that is not hollow. Even though legally in the US, "solid gold" can only be used for 24K gold, it also refers to karat gold which is not hollow or layered.

Table 2.1 Gold content and notation

Karats (USA)	Parts Gold	Gold %	Fineness (Europe & Asia)
24K	24/24	99.9%	999 or 1000
22K	22/24	91.6%	916 or 917
21K	21/24	87.5%	875
18K	18/24	75.0%	750
15K	15/24	62.5%	625
14K	14/24	58.3%	583 or 585
12K	12/24	50.0%	500
10K	10/24	41.6%	416 or 417
9K	9/24	37.5%	375
8K	8/24	33.3%	333

Platinum Content & Notation

Throughout the world, the purity of platinum is described only in terms of fineness. The markings and alloys used, however, may vary slightly. **PT**, the chemical symbol for platinum, and **PLAT** are used as abbreviated marks for platinum when identifying the metal and its fineness. For example, when 900 PT or 900 PLAT is stamped on a jewelry piece, it means that it contains at least 900 parts per thousand of pure platinum. In 1997, the U.S. Federal Trade Commission established the following guidelines for platinum markings:

Table 2.2 Platinum content and notation

Pure platinum content	Notations or marks allowed
950 parts or more per thousand of pure platinum	**Platinum, Pt, Pt., Plat, Plat**. The numerical platinum content is not required.
850 to 950 parts per thousand	**950 Plat, 950 Pt, 900 Plat, 900 Pt, 850 Plat, or 850 Pt.** The numerical platinum content must be indicated.
500 parts per thousand of platinum and at least 950 parts per 1000 platinum group metals (iridium, osmium, palladium, rhodium and ruthenium)	Can be marked with the parts per thousand of pure platinum followed by the parts per thousand of each platinum group metal (examples: **"600Plat 350Irid" or "600Pt 350Ir"**)
less than 500 parts per thousand	Cannot be marked with the word platinum or any abbreviation thereof

In Canada, "**PLATINE**" (the French word for platinum) may also be used as a mark to indicate that an article contains at least 95% platinum.

Terms Related to Metals and Imitation Gold

Base metal   A nonprecious metal such as copper, nickel or zinc

Brass   An alloy of copper and zinc

Bronze   An alloy of copper and tin

Gold electroplating   A quick and inexpensive way to make base metal look like gold. The object is dipped in a gold plating solution and then an electrical current is used to coat the object with a thin layer of gold. The thickness of the gold depends upon the amount and duration of the current. For an item to be called **gold electroplate** (commonly stamped **GEP**) in the US, the gold layer must be at least 7/1,000,000 of an inch thick. If the layer is thinner, then the item is described as **gold flashed** or **gold washed**.

Fig. 2.1 24K—24 karat gold mark.

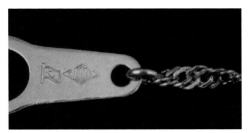

Fig. 2.2 Japanese hallmark next to fineness 1000 (quality) mark for the same chain as in fig. 2.1

Fig. 2.3 Trademark & symbol showing the design is copyrighted by Varna Platinum

Fig. 2.4 Platinum 900 fineness mark and trademark of Gelin & Abaci

Fig 8.5 Fineness mark for 14K—585

Fig. 8.6 Fineness mark for 10K—417

Fig 8.7 Poorly stamped piece, 18K—750

Fig.8.8 "18KP" means 18K plumb gold, not plated gold

Fig. 8.9 "Karat" abbreviated "ct" on an Australian piece

Fig. 8.10 Mark for 12K gold filled

All photos this page by the author

Table 2.3 lists the Mohs hardness of some pure metals. Gold, silver and platinum are alloyed to make them harder and more resistant to wear.

Table 2.3 Mohs hardness of *pure* metals

Metal	Mohs hardness	Metal	Mohs hardness
Gold	2.5 to 3	Titanium	6
Silver	2.5 to 3	Rhodium	6
Copper	3	Iridium	6.5
Platinum	4 to 4.5	Tungsten	7.5

The above Mohs hardness values are from Wikipedia and the American Federation of Mineralogical Societies.

Metal Terms (continued)

Platinum group metals (PGM) Platinum and the five other metals which are chemically and physically similar and which are often deposited with it: palladium, iridium, osmium, rhodium and ruthenium.

Pewter A tin alloy. According to the US Federal Trade commission, pewter consists of at least 90 percent tin. In colonial America, pewter was an alloy of tin and lead. Today in England, "pewter" generally refers to a tin alloy made of 91% tin, 7% antimony and 2% copper. Elsewhere it may contain other elements such as lead, bismuth and zinc, and the percentages may vary.

Precious metals Gold, silver and the platinum group metals

Rolled gold plate (RGP) Same as gold overlay. An example of how it might be indicated on a jewelry piece is **"1/40 12 Kt RGP,"** meaning that the piece has been mechanically bonded with a layer of 12K gold which is 1/40th of the total weight of the piece. Canadian law does not allow plated items to be stamped. Rolled gold plate may also be called simply "gold plate (GP)."

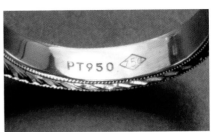

Fig. 2.11 "Plat" by itself indicates the ring has 95% pure platinum. The 750 fineness mark means the piece also has 18K gold.

Fig. 2.12 The platinum part has a fineness of 950 and the gold portion, a fineness of 750—18K.

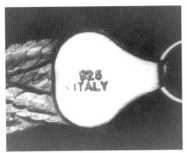

Fig. 2.13 Sterling silver mark "925" on the clasp of a bracelet

Fig. 2.14 You can tell this is not real gold by noticing the grey areas where gold plating has worn away.

Fig. 2.15 14K gold-testing acid on a penny, a sterling silver charm, a 10K heart pendant, and 18K gold. The acid on the 18K gold remained clear; whereas it turned brown, green or dark gray on the other metals. Acid testing is one of the best ways to detect fake gold and identify metals.

All photos this page by the author

Tensile strength	A metal's ability to withstand the stress of stretching. It's determined by the amount of force required to break a specified unit area of a wire of the material. Platinum alloys are generally stronger than white gold, which in turn is normally stronger than sterling silver.
Vermeil	Sterling silver covered with at least 120/millionths of an inch of fine gold. The layer of gold may be either electroplated or mechanically bonded.

Weights, Measures, and Marks

Avoirdupois weight	The weight system used in the U.S. for food and people and almost everything except precious metals and gems. One avoirdupois pound equals 16 ounces.
Carat	A unit of weight for gems, which was standardized internationally in 1913 and adapted to the metric system, with one carat equaling 1/5 of a gram. The term "carat" sounds more impressive and is easier to use than fractions of grams. Consequently, it is the preferred unit of weight for gemstones.
Grain	A measurement of weight equaling 1/24 of a pennyweight. This was one of the earliest units of weight for gold. It was originally the equivalent of one grain of wheat.
Gram	The most widespread unit of weight for gold jewelry. See Table 3.1 for equivalent weights.
Pennyweight	Unit of weight equaling 1/20 of a troy ounce. In the Middle Ages it was the weight of a silver penny in Britain. Now pennyweight is used mainly in the American jewelry trade.
Hallmark	An official mark stamped on gold, silver or platinum objects to indicate their quality, origin and maker. The term refers to the Goldsmith's Hall in London, which has overseen the marking of gold in England since 1300. Hallmarking systems are found in European countries such as Belgium, France, Britain, Germany, Holland,

Italy, Portugal and Denmark. Figure 2.16 is an example of a British hallmark.

Fig. 2.16 A British hallmark. From left to right is the maker's mark, the British-made standard mark, the purity numbers, the assay office mark, and the year letter. *Diagram reprinted with permission from the Gemological Institute of America.*

"Hallmark" also has a more general meaning which refers to any mark stamped on an article of trade to indicate origin, purity or genuineness. For example, the Japanese flag stamped on the 24K gold clasp in figure 2.2 signifies that the piece was inspected and meets Japanese standards for the quality mark of 1000 (24K gold).

Quality mark A set of numbers, letters, or symbols stamped on metal to indicate its type and content (figs. 2.1 to 2.13). For example 18K means 75% gold, 900 Plat. means 90% platinum. In the US, jewelry which does not cross state lines has not been required to have a quality mark. Fineness and karat marks are quality marks.

Tael Chinese gold weight. 1 tael=1.2034 ounces troy of 0.999 fineness.

Trademark A mark that indicates the manufacturer, importer or seller of an item (whoever stands behind its quality mark) (figs. 2.3 & 2.4). In the USA, trademarks must be registered with the Patent and Trademark Office, and trademarked items must have a quality mark. In addition, any item that bears a quality mark should have a US registered trademark. There is little enforcement of this law, however. Consequently, many types of jewelry marked 10K, 14K or 18K are not trademarked.

Troy ounce   The standard unit of weight for gold. It may have been named after a weight used at the annual fair at Troyes in France during the Middle Ages.

Specific gravity (SG)   A measure that indicates the relative density and weight of a substance. It's the ratio that compares the weight of a substance to the weight of an equal volume of water at 4°C (39°F). Pure platinum, for example, has an SG of 21.4, meaning that it's 21.4 times heavier than an equal volume of water. Pure gold has an SG of 19.3, but when it's alloyed with 25% palladium, it's SG decreases to 15.6. Pure silver has an SG of 10.6.

Troy weight   The system of weights used in the US and England for gold and silver in which one pound equals twelve ounces and one ounce equals twenty pennyweights. It should not be confused with avoirdupois weight.

Table 2.4 Weight Conversion Table

Unit of weight	Converted weight
1 pennyweight	= 1.555 g = 0.05 oz t = 0.055 oz av =
1 troy ounce (oz t)	= 31.103 g = 1.097 oz av = 20 dwt =
1 ounce	= 28.3495 g = 0.911 oz t = 18.229 dwt
1 carat (ct)	= 0.2 g = 0.006 oz t = 0.007 oz av =
1 gram (g)	= 5 cts = 0.032 oz t = 0.035 oz av =

Miscellaneous Terms

Findings   Metal components used for jewelry construction or repair such as clasps, settings, studs and safety chains.

Mounting   The metal part of a jewelry piece before the stones are set into it.

Refining   The process of removing impurities from a precious metal.

Shank   The part of a ring that encircles the finger and is attached to the stone setting(s).

Solder   A metal or metallic alloy used to join metals. Solder is designed to melt at a lower temperature than the metal to be joined. The terms **easy**, **medium**, and **hard solders** are used to describe solders with progressively higher melting points. Normally, hard solder is first used on a piece since it melts at the highest temperature. Medium and then easy solders are used afterwards. This technique permits the jeweler to solder a piece together without melting previously made joints.

Soldering   The process of uniting two pieces of heated metal together with fusible flux agents (solder). The two metal pieces remain solid and do not reach the melting point.

Welding   The process of fusing two pieces of the same alloy by heating and allowing the metals to flow together.

Which is Better—14K or 18K Gold?

You may wonder whether 14K or 18K gold is better. 18K rings have 3/4 gold and 1/4 other material whereas 14K is just a little more than half gold. Consequently, rings with 18K gold are more valuable. They're also less likely to cause a reaction in people who are allergic to metals alloyed with gold, and they usually have a deeper yellow color than 14K gold. However, some 18K gold alloys may not be as hard and strong as 14K gold.

Rings of 14K gold are less expensive and often wear better. In North America, you'll probably have a better selection of 14K jewelry because a greater variety of it is manufactured. However, 14K might have a tendency to discolor or tarnish due to the lower percentage of gold and high percentage of copper. Occasionally, the metals alloyed with 14K gold cause an allergic reaction in some people. Nickel white gold alloys are the ones most likely to cause allergic reactions. (White gold is often made by alloying pure gold with metals such as silver, copper, nickel and palladium. Rose gold is made by alloying it primarily with copper.

Much of the better jewelry is made in 18K gold, palladium or platinum. More and more jewelry of 22K, 24K or 990 gold is becoming

17

available. This higher-karat gold is hypoallergenic and resists tarnish, and some of the new alloys are relatively durable. If you have a ring custom made, you can choose the gold percentage.

Have a look at some 14K, 18K and higher-karat gold rings. Usually there's some difference in color. Consider your color preferences along with the above points when choosing the karat quality. More often than not, the determining factor will be whether or not you can find a ring you like in your price range.

Silver Jewelry

Many cultures have associated silver with the moon and gold with the sun. Both metals have symbolized wealth and prosperity and are said to intensify the spiritual and healing powers of gems. After the discovery of the Americas by the Europeans, so much silver was mined in Central and South America that the value attached to silver fell sharply. This led to the conversion of most monetary systems to the gold standard.

Today Mexico, Peru, Australia, the United States, Canada, and the former USSR are the leading producers of silver. The primary source of silver is its recovery as a byproduct of lead, copper, gold or zinc production. To increase the sale of silver jewelry, manufacturers have positioned it to compete with fashion jewelry, rather than competing with fine jewelry in gold, platinum and palladium. Nevertheless prestigious jewelers offer silver jewelry created by some of the world's top designers. Most craft jewelry is made from silver.

Pure silver, like pure gold and platinum, is too soft for most jewelry use so it is often alloyed with other metal(s). Copper is normally preferred because it improves the metal's hardness and durability without detracting from the bright shine characteristic of silver. However, even alloyed silver does not provide settings as secure as those of white gold, platinum and palladium alloys.

Sterling silver is the alloy most commonly used in jewelry making and silversmithing. It consists of 92.5% silver and 7.5% copper. It was adopted as a standard alloy in England in the 12th century. Usually sterling silver is identified with its fineness marking of **925**. Other acceptable markings on sterling are "ster.," "sterling," and "sterling silver."

Fig. 2.17 A Mexican silver bracelet from Joseph DuMouchelle Auctioneers. *Photo by David Frechette.*

Fig. 2.19 Sterling silver 925 mark and trademark on back of pendant in fig 2.18. *Photo by author.*

Fig. 2.18 Sterling silver pendant hand crafted by Shawna Whiteside. *Photo by author.*

Fig. 2.20 Sterling silver cuff. *Handmade and photographed by Tom DeGasperis of Dancing Designs.*

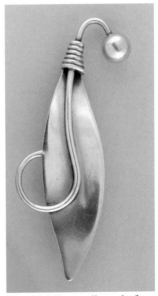

Fig. 2.21 Taxco silver pin from Joseph DuMouchelle Auctioneers. *Photo by David Frechette.*

Another common alloy that contains 10% to 20% copper is called coin silver. In Europe, alloys with 80%, 83%, and 87.5% are also used and are called European or Continental silver. An alloy popular in the Far East uses 90% silver and 10% zinc.

In Peru, a high percentage of jewelry is made with alloys of 95% silver and stamped 950. Flatware and hollowware in France has been made out of 950 silver, and some silversmiths in the silver center of Taxco, Mexico have used 950 silver alloys. Occasionally when people see the 950 stamp, they assume that the metal is platinum. Look for "pt" or "plat" next to the "950" stamp to determine if it's a platinum stamp.

Silver jewelry sold at street vendors can have varying degrees of fineness, sometimes lower than standard qualities, making it difficult to repair and size the jewelry. Therefore, if you buy rings from tourist vendors, make sure they fit and don't need to be resized.

A disadvantage of most silver alloys is that they tarnish. Tarnish-resistant silver, is available, but the supply is limited and the cost may be about ten percent more than that of sterling silver. Peter Johns, a silversmith in England, discovered in the1990's that the addition of germanium to silver could make it resistant to tarnish and firestain. (Germanium is a silver-white element chemically similar to tin; firestain is a dark coating that forms on silver when the metal oxidizes at high temperatures.) This tarnish-free silver is patented and sold under the trade name Argentium™

Other tarnish resistant alloys have been created by replacing the 7.5% copper in sterling silver with materials such as platinum, silicon or nickel. The presence of copper in sterling silver accelerates tarnishing, so when copper is omitted, the resulting silver alloy is more tarnish resistant. However, it also tends to be softer than and not as strong as sterling silver made with copper. Tarnish-resistant silver is often sold as "tarnish-free" silver, but this can be misleading. Any silver product can tarnish over the long term.

Another way to make silver tarnish-resistant is to plate it with rhodium. This plated silver usually costs less than silver alloyed with metals other than copper, but the plating can wear away. The resulting exposed metal can tarnish. If your goal is to buy unplated silver that is inherently tarnish resistant, ask first if the silver is plated or not.

Silver jewelry is reasonably priced, versatile and the most reflective of all the precious metals. Silver can go with any outfit; it can be casual, yet worn with dressy clothes. However, silver is facing competition from other affordable white metals. They are discussed in the next section.

Other White Metals Used for Jewelry

In May 2001, platinum was selling for about $600 an ounce. Five years later in 2006, platinum prices had doubled to more than $1200 an ounce. High platinum prices have prompted designers and manufacturers to expand jewelry lines using other white metals—the precious metal palladium and the non-precious metals titanium, stainless steel and tungsten. Information about these four metals is provided in this section in order to help you determine which jewelry metals best fit your needs.

Palladium

Palladium, a member of the platinum group metals, offers many of the advantages of platinum but weighs only 56% as much, making large pieces more comfortable to wear, especially earrings and necklaces. (The specific gravity of palladium is 12.2 compared to 21.4 of platinum.) The lower density and weight of palladium also allows for chunkier and taller designs that are still affordable.

Palladium pieces are also more affordable because the price of palladium has come down significantly from what it was around 2001. Like all metals, the price of palladium will fluctuate. During 2006, for example, palladium ranged from around $250–$350 an ounce, only about half the price of pure gold and one-fourth the price of platinum.

Palladium is a little softer than platinum. However the durability depends on the alloy used and the manufacturing process. Machine-made (die-struck) settings are usually more durable than those that are cast.

Like platinum, palladium has the following advantages. Palladium:

◆ Resists tarnish, doesn't discolor the skin or turn yellowish with wear

◆ Is malleable, making it easy to form and manipulate. It doesn't have the brittleness of white gold.

◆ Is hypoallergenic

Fig. 2.22 Palladium bridal rings by Art Carved®. *Photo from PAI (Palladium Alliance International).*

Fig. 2.23 Platinum diamond ring from Abe Mor Diamond Cutters & Co. *Photo by KD Imaging.*

Fig. 2.24 950 palladium, tourmaline, sapphire and diamond ring from Mann Design Group. *Design by Lainie Mann. Photo by Mark Mann.*

Fig. 2.25 Palladium and diamond ring. *Ring and photo from Mark Schneider.*

♦ Is whiter than white gold. Palladium is about the same color as platinum but slightly darker and more grayish than platinum. The color depends on the alloy used. When the consumers see palladium next to platinum jewelry, they usually think it looks the same. Sometimes palladium is rhodium plated to make it brighter, but this is not necessary.

♦ Outwears white gold

♦ Is classified as a precious metal with an inherent commodity value

♦ Often has a high purity (95%). It's typically alloyed with other hypoallergenic platinum-group metals such as ruthenium, and bears a fineness stamp of 950 when it contains 95% palladium. This higher purity increases its value.

With all these advantages, you may wonder why palladium has only recently been promoted as an ideal jewelry metal. It wasn't until 1803 that palladium was isolated and identified as a separate elemental metal by a researcher named William Hyde Wollaston. He named his discovery after the asteroid Pallas, which was in turn named after the Greek Goddess of Wisdom.

Palladium, however, was quite rare until in 1930 when the International Nickel Company of Canada began producing it in significant quantities. It was used for gold alloys, especially in dentistry. During World War II, it was used as an alternative to platinum, which was declared a strategic metal. Starting in the 1970's, palladium was in demand for catalytic converters and for electronic circuitry, but because of its low supply and high price relative to other metals, it was seldom promoted as a jewelry metal. In early 2001, the price of palladium reached a high of $1090 per ounce, higher than the price of platinum at the time. Fortunately there have been new finds of palladium in Montana, Canada and Zimbabwe, which have increased supply and brought down prices below those of gold and platinum. As a result, it makes sense to take advantage of palladium's benefits and promote it as a distinctive jewelry metal.

In March 2006, the Palladium Alliance International (PAI) organization was formed to position palladium as a luxurious jewelry metal. PAI provides education, marketing and technical support to the trade and general public. It has offices in Billings, Montana, and Shanghai, China. PAI's website is www.luxurypalladium.com.

Titanium

People who want sturdy, comfortable jewelry are attracted to titanium. Its exceptional strength and light weight make it ideal not only for the aerospace industry but also for rings and watches, which must be able to withstand a lot of wear. Titanium was first discovered in 1791 but wasn't commercially available until the 1940's, when a refining process for it was invented by William J. Kroll. It's been used for jewelry since the 1980's and is becoming increasingly popular.

Titanium:

♦ Is very durable and doesn't dent easily or get deformed, so it's a good choice for people who work out or engage in sports.

♦ Resists tarnish, doesn't discolor the skin or turn yellowish with wear

♦ Is hypoallergenic

♦ Is low-priced. Titanium jewelry normally sells for less than that made of white gold.

♦ Weighs less than other jewelry metals (specific gravity: 4.506)

♦ Has a high purity, usually ranging from 90 to 99 percent pure

♦ With an electrical charge, can be colored bright colors such as blue and purple, a process called anodizing

♦ Does not require rhodium plating to maintain its color or make it scratch resistant

Like all metals, titanium has a few drawbacks. Its exceptional strength and resistance to bending prevent it from being used for prong and bezel settings. Its hardness wears down jewelry-making tools very quickly. Titanium cannot be soldered and it can't be sized more than one-half size. This can be a problem, if you'd like to wear the same wedding ring for a lifetime. Size adjustments of plus-two sizes are not uncommon during one's life.

A wide variety of styles are available in titanium, including prong and bezel settings made with gold or platinum and inlays of metal or gemstones like black onyx. Titanium can also be textured with different finishes.

Titanium metal comes in different grades. The strongest grade is aircraft grade 6-4, which consists of 6% aluminum, 4% vanadium and used for jewelry as well as for hip implants, but it's not as strong as most

Fig. 2.26 Titanium and diamonds with 14K yellow gold accents. *Bracelet & photo from The Bell Group Rio Grande.*

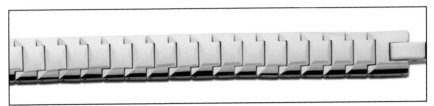

Fig. 2.27 Tungsten bracelet. *Jewelry and photo from The Bell Group Rio Grande.*

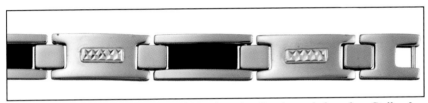

Fig. 2.28 Stainless steel, 14K gold and onyx bracelet. *Jewelry and photo from Stuller, Inc.*

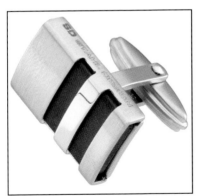

Fig. 2.30 Titanium and sterling silver inlay band. *Ring and photo from The Bell Group Rio Grande.*

Fig. 2.29 Stainless steel & black rubber cuff link. *Link & photo from Stuller, Inc.*

90% titanium. Commercially pure titanium (also called Ti999) is also used for jewelry as well as for hip implants, but it's not as strong as most titanium alloys Because of its high durability, titanium jewelry is especially popular with men. Women's jewelry is also available.

Stainless Steel

Stainless steel watches have played a major role in the growth of stainless steel jewelry. Some men who would never consider wearing a gold or platinum bracelet, will buy one of steel to go with their watch. Men will also accessorize their watches with stainless steel pendants, wedding rings and necklaces. Women also buy stainless steel jewelry, particularly in Europe, where they are the primary buyers.

Steel is an iron alloy containing about 0.5 to 1.5 percent carbon. **Stainless steel** is steel alloyed with at least 10 to 13 percent chromium for corrosion resistance (sources differ on the percentage of chromium required). Nickel may also be added to increase corrosion resistance. "Surgical stainless steel" is mainly a marketing term and does not refer to one type or grade of steel.

It's not easy to characterize stainless steel because of the wide range of different alloys. In general, most stainless steel jewelry:

♦ resists corrosion and does not discolor the skin

♦ is relatively light weight (specific gravity: 7.7 or 7.8)

♦ wears better than brass and most gold

♦ is low priced

♦ is suited to innovative finishes and creative designs

Rising platinum prices have motivated more and more jewelry manufacturers to consider stainless steel as an alternative white jewelry metal. They can buy high quality material and combine it with precious metals and gems to create attractive, affordable jewelry. You'll probably see more of it in jewelry stores in the years to come.

Tungsten

Until recently, tungsten has been primarily used in jewelry as an alloying element to increase durability. For example, platinum when alloyed with tungsten wears better and is more scratch resistant than other platinum alloys.

Fig. 2.31 Tungsten rings. *Photo and rings from Heavy Stone Rings.*

In Scandinavian, tungsten means heavy stone (tung sten). Tungsten was discovered in 1783 by Jose and Fausto Elhuyar and is sometimes referred to as "Wolfram," which is why its chemical symbol is W.

All tungsten rings are a combination of elements, usually tungsten and carbon, which forms a compound called tungsten carbide. This alloy is so strong that it's used in place of diamond for cutting tools. The jewelry industry usually refers to tungsten carbide as tungsten and the industrial industry refers to it as carbide.

27

Unlike titanium or stainless steel, tungsten is a heavy metal (specific gravity: 19.62), giving it a similar feel to platinum.

Like titanium, tungsten:

♦ Is very durable and doesn't dent easily or get deformed, so it's a good choice for people who work out or engage in sports.

♦ Does not discolor skin or turn yellowish with wear.

♦ Is hypoallergenic except for some tungsten carbide jewelry, which may contain the element cobalt and cause allergic reactions in some people.

♦ Is low-priced, although some rings retail for as much as $1000. Tungsten jewelry generally costs more than titanium jewelry because of the difference in equipment and environmental control needed to produce it. For both metals, labor costs are normally higher than the metal itself. Special skills and equipment are required.

♦ Does not require rhodium plating to maintain its color or make it scratch resistant. The color, however, can vary depending on the grade of tungsten used.

♦ Can be combined with gold or platinum for interesting designs

Tungsten carbide rings cannot be resized, but sometimes a company will replace the ring free of charge if a new size is required.

However, these drawbacks to tungsten may not matter to an active person who's hard on jewelry. If you're looking for durable, scratch resistant pieces similar in weight to gold or platinum, then tungsten jewelry could be the right choice for you.

3

Basic Facts About Gems

This chapter presents basic gem terminology and describes gem shapes and cutting styles in order to help you understand gemstone descriptions on invoices and in this book. It also lists birthstones and anniversary stones.

Gemstone Terms Defined

Facets	The polished surfaces or planes on a stone. Normally they are flat, but some cutters are now creating stones with concave facets. Facets are intended to create brilliance in a gemstone.
Table	The large, flat top facet. It normally has an octagonal shape on a round stone.
Girdle	The narrow rim around the stone. The girdle plane is the largest diameter of any part of the stone.
Crown	The upper part of the stone above the girdle
Pavilion	The lower part of the stone below the girdle
Culet	The tiny facet on the pointed bottom of the pavilion, parallel to the table. Sometimes the point of a stone is called "the culet" even if no culet facet is present.
Fancy Shape	Any shape except round. This term is most frequently applied to diamonds.
Rough	Gem material in its natural state as it comes out of the ground prior to cutting or polishing
Critical angle	The angle at which the majority of the light is reflected back into the stone. Cutting below this angle creates a window (see-through-the-stone) effect. The angle varies from one gemstone mineral to another.

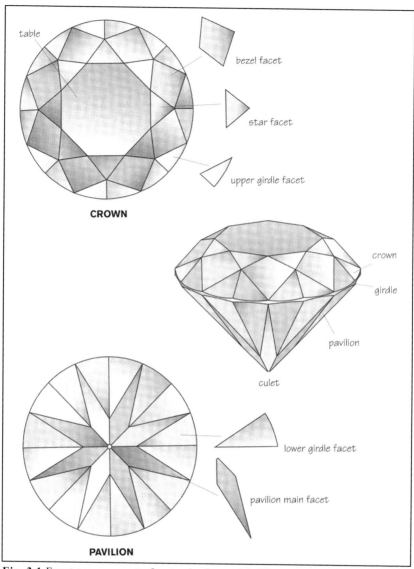

Fig. 3.1 Facet arrangement of a standard round brilliant cut. *Diagram reprinted with permission from the Gemological Institute of America.*

Shape Versus Cutting Style

When gemologists speak of a gem's *shape*, they usually mean its face-up outline. The most common gemstone shapes include the round, oval, square, triangle, pear, marquise, heart and **cushion**, a squarish or rectangular shape with curved sides and rounded corners.

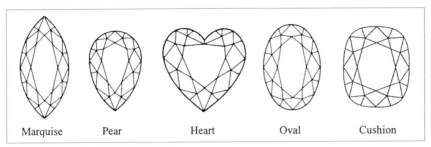

| Marquise | Pear | Heart | Oval | Cushion |

Fig. 3.2 Common gemstone shapes

Gems can be any geometric shape or they may resemble things such as animals, bells, stars, the moon, etc. They can also be cut as abstract freeforms.

Cutting style refers to the way in which a stone is cut or faceted. An oval-shaped stone, for example, may just be rounded as a cabochon or it may have facets (polished surfaces with varying shapes) that are arranged in different styles. The term *emerald cut* has a double meaning. It indicates that the shape is square or rectangular with clipped-off corners and that the faceting style is a step cut, which has parallel rows of long, four-sided facets. A **radiant cut** has the same shape as an emerald cut but has facets similar to those of a round brilliant cut

Fig. 3.3 Emerald cut. *Photo by author.*

Fig. 3.4 Radiant cut. *Photo by author.*

Traditional Cutting Styles

Before the 1300's, gems were usually cut into unfaceted rounded beads or into cabochons (unfaceted dome-shaped stones). Colored gems looked attractive cut this way, but diamonds looked dull. Thanks to man's interest in bringing out the beauty of diamonds, the art of faceting gemstones was developed. At first, facets were added haphazardly, but

by around 1450, diamonds began to be cut with a
symmetrical arrangement of facets. The first
symmetrical style probably evolved out of the
natural octahedral shape of some diamond crystals.
Simply by flattening one point or cutting it off, a
table facet was formed. This created a symmetrical style called the **table
cut**, which had a crown, pavilion and nine facets (ten if there were a
culet). More complex styles gradually emerged, and there were advances
in cutting tools and technology. One of the most important develop-
ments was the introduction of the rotary diamond saw around 1900. By
the 1920's, the modern round-brilliant cut had become popular.

Fig. 3.5 Table cut

As cutters discovered how faceting could bring out the brilliance
and sparkle of diamonds, they started to apply the same techniques to
colored stones. Today, gems are cut into the following basic styles:

Cabochon Cut Has a dome-shaped top and either a flat
or rounded bottom. This is the simplest
cut for a stone and is often seen in
antique jewelry. Today this cutting style
tends to be used for opaque, translucent, and star or
cat's-eye stones, but transparent material is also used.
Sometimes stones are cut as a cabochon on top and
faceted on the bottom to add some brilliance. Since
the **cabochon** is the simplest style, it costs less to cut
than faceted styles.

Cabochon

Step Cut Has rows of facets that resemble the steps of a staircase.
The facets are usually four-sided and elongated, and
parallel to the girdle. One example is the **baguette**, a
rectangular square-cornered stone. If step-cuts have
clipped-off corners, they're called **emerald cuts**.
Emeralds are often cut this way to protect the corners and
provide places where prongs can secure the stone.

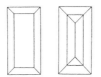

Fig. 3.6 Step-cut baguette

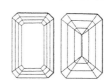

Fig. 3.7 Emerald cut

Gemstone Cutting Stages

Fig. 3.8 A mixed color parcel of Mahenge spinel rough from East Africa. *Photo by Clay Zava.*

Fig. 3.9 Preforms from the previous parcel ready for dopping (affixing to a stone holder called a dop) and cutting. *Photo by Clay Zava.*

Fig. 3.10 Layout of a small parcel of fine red and pink spinel. *Gems and photo by Clay Zava.*

Fig. 3.11 Completed pavilions (bottoms) of peridot, garnet & spinel. *Gems & photo by C. Zava.*

Fig. 3.12 Aligning the facets of a 90-carat emerald-cut golden beryl, in preparation for cutting and polishing the crown. *Photo by Clay Zava.*

Fig. 3.13 Gemcutter Clay Zava at work. *Photo by Bill Patty.*

Brilliant Cut Has mostly 3-sided facets which radiate outward from the stone. Kite- or lozenge-shaped facets may be present. The best-known example is the **full-cut round brilliant**, which has 58 facets. Ovals, pears, marquises, and heart-shapes can also be brilliant-cut. The **single cut**, which has 17 or 18 facets, is another type of brilliant cut. Square stones cut in the brilliant style are called **princess cuts**. Triangular brilliant cuts are called **trilliants**.. Brilliant-style facets create a greater amount of brilliance and sparkle than step facets do. Gemstone pendants or earrings are occasionally cut as **briolettes**. These have a tear-drop shape, a circular cross-section and brilliant-style facets (or occasionally rectangular, step-cut-style facets or else no facets).

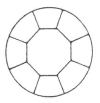

Fig. 3.14 Single Cut

Mixed cut Has both step- and brilliant-cut facets. This is a popular faceting style for colored stones. The crown is brilliant-cut to maximize brilliance and hide flaws if present. The pavilion, on the other hand, is either entirely step cut or else has a combination of both step- and brilliant-type facets. The step facets allow cutters to save weight and bring out the color of the stone. Occasionally, the mixed cut is referred to as the **Ceylon cut**.

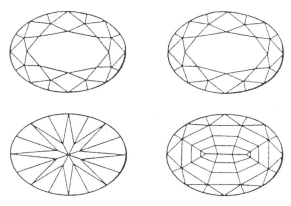

Fig. 3.15 Brilliant cut oval   **Fig. 3.16** Mixed cut oval

Fig. 3.17 Oval brilliant-cut diamond, half-moon brilliant cut, and small round brilliant cuts. *Ring from J. Landau Inc.; photo by Derse Studio.*

Fig. 3.18 Mixed-cut sapphire, round brilliant cut diamonds and a close-up view of granulation on a 22-karat gold ring by Zaffiro. *Photo by Daniel Van Rossen.*

Fig. 3.19 Sapphire cabochon and round brilliant-cut diamonds. *Ring by Andrew Sarosi; photo by Rachelle Sarosi.*

Fig 3.20 Emerald-cut Afghan tourmaline cut by Clay Zava. *Photo: Robert Weldon.*

Bead **(faceted & unfaceted)** Usually has a ball-shaped form with a hole through the center. Most faceted beads have either brilliant- or step-type facets. Today, beads are generally made from lower-priced material. High-quality rubies and emeralds, for example, are usually faceted. It would be pointless to lower their weight and value by drilling holes through them.

Step-cut bead

Fig. 3.21 Twisted strands of faceted and unfaceted beads of amber, grossular garnet, freshwater pearls, tiger's eye, peridot, jasper, citrine and handmade gold beads. The 22k pendant/enhancer/brooch features a tourmaline and South Sea pearl with citrine accent stones. *Design copyright 2006 by Carolyn Tyler; photo by R & R Photography.*

History and Significance of the Bead

Beads were one of the initial indicators of human development. In fact, they predated rock art. The first beads were made of organic materials such as bone, teeth, shell, wood, seeds and nuts, many of which decomposed. Some pierced shells, however, have withstood the trials of time and date back as far as 100,000 to 135,000 years.

Beads have served many functions. They've been used as:

♦ **Protective charms** and religious objects
♦ **Social markers** of ethnic and individual identity, including age, marital status, rank or position, accomplishments, etc.
♦ **Currency** and indicators of wealth
♦ A form of **ornamentation**
♦ A **means of communication**, as in South Africa, for example, where young Zulu women create beaded "love letters" to give to a young man. The message is encoded in the colors and occasionally in words.

A "bead" is more than an ornament with a hole in it that can be strung. It requires a human connection and in fact is a tracer of humanity from caveman to present day. The bead has always been there. We humans seem to have a need or desire for this tactile, personal object.

In archeology, it has become a "technological" and cultural indicator. For example, many ancient civilizations/cities are close to mines and other sources of bead materials; evidence has also shown that many bead finds are from a source far away from the place being excavated. These discoveries reveal not only the technological capabilities of various societies but even trade networks, some of which surprised the scientists and have led to new realizations of the pervasiveness of early trade. For millennia, the bead was the most common trade object, placed in ships as ballast and carried to the far corners of the world. This fact has assisted researchers in tracking human migration.

The above Information is from Sindi Schloss, a jewelry appraiser and educator, and associate curator at the Bead Museum in Glendale, Arizona.

Sometimes stones are not cut, but simply used in their original state as rough crystals. The ring in figure 3.22 has a perfect octahedral diamond crystal specimen flanked by two **macles** (twinned crystals, which are typically triangular and flattened in shape.) Crystal jewelry is not only worn for its distinctive beauty but also for psychic and healing purposes.

Fig. 3.22 Diamond octahedron and macle crystals. *Ring by Todd Reed; photo by Azadphoto.com.*

Fig. 3.23 Green beryl and yellow sapphire crystals in jewelry by Robert Wander for Winc Creations. *Photo courtesy of JQ Magazine.*

Non-Traditional Cuts

The traditional round, oval, pear, emerald, marquise and cushion shapes can have non-traditional cutting styles. For example, they may have concave facets instead of flat ones; they may be faceted on the top or bottom and carved on the other side; or they may be entirely carved. These non-traditional styles are loosely called **fantasy cuts**. However, this term can also refer to gemstones with non-traditional shapes, such as stars, shields, triangles, leaves, etc. They may also have free-form, one-of a kind shapes; and the cutting styles may be traditional or not. The best way to learn about non-traditional cuts is to look at examples. Some are shown below and on the next two pages.

Fig. 3.24 Ripple Top™ unheated aquamarine. *Cut & photographed by John D. Dyer.*

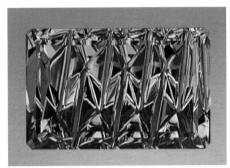

Fig. 3.25 Pink tourmaline ZigZag™ cut. *Created and photographed by John D. Dyer.*

Fig. 3.26 Malaya garnet Dreamscape™ cut. *Created & photographed by John D. Dyer.*

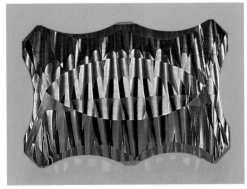

Fig. 3.27 Amethyst concave cut with scalloped outline. *Cut and photographed by John D. Dyer.*

Fig. 3.28 Dahlia-cut Afghan tourmaline fashioned by Clay Zava. *Photo by Robert Weldon.*

Fig. 3.29 Blue-green tourmaline Vortex™ cut. *Created and photographed by John D. Dyer.*

Fig. 3.30 Citrine Radial Ray™ cut. *Created and photographed by John D. Dyer.*

Fig. 3.31 Fire opal pin/pendant created, carved, and photographed by Angela Conty.

Fig. 3.32 Hand-carved ametrine and rock crystal quartz orchid. *Pendant and photo by Tom DeGasperis.*

Fig. 3.33 Namibian blue druse chalcedony cut by Dieter Lorenz, set with a freshwater pearl. *Pin by Fred & Kate Pearce; photo by Ralph Gabriner.*

Fig. 3.34 "Optic dish" amethyst cut by Michael Dyber, set with red spinels. *Pendant Fred Pearce; Photo: Ralph Gabriner.*

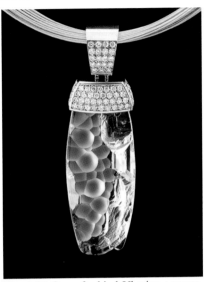

Fig. 3.35 One-of-a-kind Ukraine aquamarine carved by Lucas Schweizer. *Pendant by Barbara Westwood; photo by Sky Hall.*

Fig. 3.36 Black drusy quartz carving by Larry Woods. *Pendant & photo by Tom DeGasperis of Dancing Designs.*

Fig. 3.37 Rubellite carved by Sherris Cottier Shank. *Photo: Robert Weldon.*

Test your gem IQ

Fig. 3.38 Can you guess what type of gems these are? See end of chapter for the answer. *Gemstones cut by Clay Zava; photo by Robert Weldon..*

Birthstones and Anniversary Stones

The belief that a special gemstone was associated with each month of the year probably originated during the first century. The development of this belief was influenced by two references in the Bible—the twelve stones of Aaron's ceremonial breastplate, described in Exodus 28:15-21 and the foundation stones of the new Jerusalem discussed in Revelation 21:19-20.

For centuries gemstones had often been used for their therapeutic virtues. Different diseases required different stones for healing. People also used gems to ward off evil spirits and to serve as religious symbols. Apparently, though, it wasn't until the eighteenth century in Poland that people started wearing their birthstone or zodiac stone in order to bring good luck. Once people started wearing birthstones, it became an established tradition. The owners of birthstone jewelry liked the idea of wearing something associated with their month of birth and personality.

Depending on which source you read, the birthstone list can vary because different cultures have selected the stones most meaningful to them. One of the best references is *The Curious Lore of Precious Stones* by George Frederick Kunz, Chapter IX. This book provides several lists of birthstones, including the one adopted by the National Association of Jewelers at their meeting in August 1912 in Kansas City. It's given on the next page and is the birthstone list most commonly used in North America. A few stones have been added based on changes or additions made later by jewelry organizations.

Birthstones

January	Garnet
February	Amethyst
March	Bloodstone or aquamarine
April	Diamond
May	Emerald
June	Pearl, moonstone or alexandrite
July	Ruby
August	Peridot or sardonyx
September	Sapphire
October	Opal or tourmaline
November	Topaz
December	Turquoise, zircon, lapis lazuli or tanzanite

Jewelers and gem dealers have also developed an anniversary list:

Anniversary Stones

1st	Gold jewelry or freshwater pearls
2nd	Garnet
3rd	Pearl
4th	Blue topaz
5th	Sapphire
6th	Amethyst
7th	Onyx
8th	Tourmaline
9th	Lapis lazuli
10th	Diamond jewelry
11th	Turquoise or zircon
12th	Jade or pearls
13th	Citrine
14th	Opal, gold jewelry
15th	Ruby
16th	Peridot
17th	Watches
18th	Cat's-eye, chrysoberyl
19th	Aquamarine
20th	Emerald, platinum
21st	Iolite

22nd	Spinel
23rd	Imperial topaz
24th	Tanzanite
25th	Silver
30th	Pearls
35th	Emerald, jade, or coral
40th	Ruby
45th	Sapphire
50th	Gold
55th	Alexandrite or emerald
60th	Diamond
75th	Diamond, gold

For more in-depth information on gemstones, consult the *Gemstone Buying Guide, Gem & Jewelry Pocket Guide, Pearl Buying Guide, Diamond Ring Buying Guide, Diamond Handbook*, and *Ruby, Sapphire & Emerald Buying Guide* by Renee Newman.

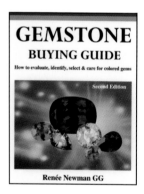
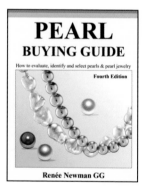
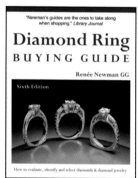

Answer to figure 3.38 question:

All of the stones are pink tanzanites (zoisites). Even gemologists would have a difficult time identifying them just from the picture, which is why they conduct a series of tests before positively identifying gems.

4

Manufacturing Methods

Suppose you're looking at two 14K solitaire rings. One was made from components punched out of solid gold by a machine, and the other was formed by casting molten gold into a mold. Which ring would probably wear better? Which ring would cost more to make?

The gold of the machine-made ring would normally be harder and denser. Therefore, it would wear better. The manufacturing cost of each ring would depend largely on the number produced. In smaller quantities, casting is definitely cheaper.

This chapter presents the four basic methods of making jewelry: casting, stamping (die-striking), electroforming, and hand fabrication. In addition, it explains the benefits of each method and how combining the methods may be advantageous when producing a piece.

Lost Wax Casting

Lost wax casting dates back to at least 1500 BC, when the Egyptians used it. For a while this method disappeared, but in recent years it has become the most widely used manufacturing process. Lost wax casting involves a series of steps, as follows:

1. **A model (jewelry piece) is made in metal** from an original design. Sometimes the model is a piece which has already been cast. (Often the first step in lost wax casting is to carve a model in wax. The rubber molding process, described in steps one to three, is relatively new compared to the modeling of wax by hand carving.)

2. **A rubber mold of the metal model is made** (fig. 4.1). The model is placed in a rectangular

Fig. 4.1 Rubber mold

frame, rubber is packed around it, the rubber is heated so it flows around the model and is vulcanized into a solid block.

3. **A wax copy(s) of the model is made** by injecting wax into the mold through a hole. An original wax model may be carved or sculpted instead (fig. 4.4). It's usually faster to carve a wax model than to make a metal model.

4. **The wax model(s) are attached to a base either in the form of a tree** (fig. 4.2) or a donut. The tree may be formed with several wax models all made from the same mold or with different-style models.

5. **The wax tree or donut is covered with a material like plaster of Paris**, called investment. This is allowed to harden.

6. **The plaster mold is heated.** The wax melts and pours out of a hole in the base. A hollow plaster mold is left.

7. **Molten gold or platinum is thrust into the plaster mold by centrifugal force or vacuum.** The open spaces left by the melted wax are filled with the metal. The gold or platinum is allowed to solidify.

8. **The hot plaster mold is plunged into water.** The sudden change of temperature makes the plaster shatter, leaving metal copies of the wax models (fig. 4.4). These are cleaned and polished.

It's best for a cast piece to be made from an original model. Detail is lost whenever a piece is recopied. Also, each time a rubber mold is made, the resulting wax and copy are a little smaller and thinner than the original.

Advantages of casting

♦ It's a relatively quick way of making several identical pieces.

♦ It offers unlimited design possibilities. You can even draw your own designs and have the jeweler transfer them to a wax model.

♦ It's economical when many pieces are produced from the same mold. One-of-a-kind cast pieces, however, can be just as costly as those which are hand-fabricated.

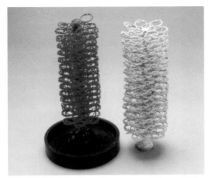

Fig. 4.2 "Tree" with wax models and the resulting gold castings. *Photo from Stamper Black Hills Gold Jewelry.*

Fig. 4.3 Wax model for casting process. *Photo and wax model by Mark Mann.*

Fig. 4.4 Finished rough casting. *Photo and ring by Mark Mann.*

Fig. 4.5 Finished palladium diamond ring. *Photo and ring by Mark Mann.*

Fig. 4.6 Wax hand-sculpted by Peggy Croft. *Photo by author.*

Fig. 4.7 The custom-designed silver and gold cast brooch made from wax model in fig 4.6. *Photo by author.*

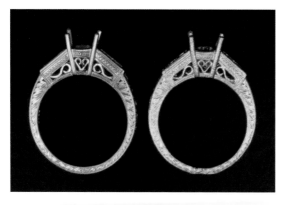

Fig. 4.8 Hand-fabricated, hand-engraved ring by Varna Platinum (left), which was used to make a mold for the cast platinum ring on the right. The hard to reach areas in the cast ring are rougher, duller and shallower. The metal in the hand-fabricated ring is denser, in contrast to the more porous cast ring; and the engraving is crisper and smoother. Normally, casting is not a good manufacturing option for fine engraved pieces.

Fig. 4.9 The difference between the hand-fabricated ring (left) and the cast ring on the right becomes more obvious when viewed close up.

All photos this page by author

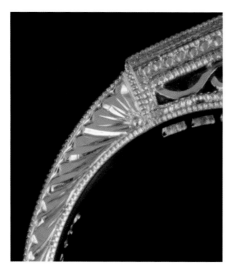

Fig. 4.10 Hand-fabricated ring by Varna viewed under a 10-power microscope.

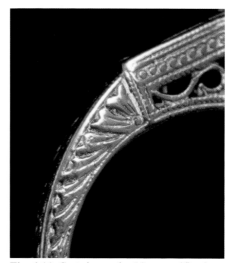

Fig. 4.11 Cast ring under 10x magnification

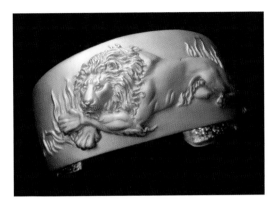

Fig. 4.12 A cast 18K gold bracelet made from a wax model carved by Peggy Croft for LRG Studio 13, Inc. Casting was an ideal manufacturing method for this piece. It's faster and easier to carve figurative designs in wax than in the metal itself. When mistakes are made, they can be easily corrected in wax, unlike metal. *Photo by author.*

♦ It's an easy way to make copies or matching pieces. For example, a necklace might be used to make a mold for a matching bracelet. A lost earring can possibly be replaced by copying the remaining earring, providing it's not too thin.

Disadvantages of casting

♦ Due to their lower density, cast pieces don't wear as well as those which are stamped and hand-fabricated.

♦ Cast gold and platinum is less suitable for fine engraving because it's more porous.

♦ Casting usually requires more cleanup and finishing than other methods. As a result, cast jewelry is often rougher and duller underneath, especially in hard to reach areas.

Stamping (Die-Striking)

Another ancient technique for making jewelry is **stamping**, which in the United States is also called **die-striking**. In this process, metal is punched between two carved metal blocks called **dies**, creating a form and design. The metal becomes very dense and strong as the hydraulic presses squeeze it between the dies at pressures of up to 25 tons per square inch.

Fig. 4-13 Die-struck ring & photo from True Knots.

The quality of stamped jewelry has greatly improved over the years. In some cases, it even looks like it's hand fabricated. The stamping process is often used to make earrings, pendants, coins, wedding bands (fig.4.13), settings, and fancy Italian chains. Its positive and negative characteristics are as follows:

Advantages of stamping

♦ Once the dies are made, it's a faster process than other methods.

♦ The quality is consistent from one piece to another. Edges are perfectly straight, and shapes are perfectly symmetrical. Consistency may also be achieved by using machines to cut and finish cast pieces.

♦ In large quantities, stamping is economical.

♦ Stamped items usually wear better than cast items, because of their high density.

♦ Stamped pieces require little cleanup before polishing.

♦ Stamped jewelry can take a very high polish due to its density.

♦ Stamped pieces can be thinner than those which are cast. Therefore, they may provide a bigger look at a lower price.

♦ Stamped gold or platinum is ideal for engraving because of its high density.

Disadvantages of Stamping

♦ It's not suitable for small-scale manufacturing because of the high cost of the dies and equipment.

♦ It's a longer process than casting if the dies are not readily available. To have dies made may take a month.

♦ Design options are limited.

Electroforming

Electroforming is a technique of forming metal objects by electrically depositing the metal over a mold. The mold, which may be made of a material such as wax, epoxy resin, or silicone rubber, is later removed, leaving a metal shell.

The process of electroforming originated in the 1830's with the birth of electroplating (Rod Edwards, *The Technique of Jewelry*, p.202). It became a convenient and extremely accurate way for museums to reproduce antique pieces. Originally, gold electroforming required a very high karat gold—at least 23.5K. But in the early 1980's, a French jewelry manufacturer developed a way of making electroformed pieces out of 14K and 18K gold. Since then, electroformed jewelry has become increasingly popular.

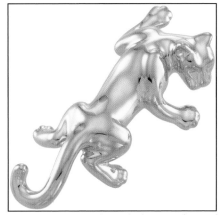

Fig. 4.14 Electroformed pin. *Jewelry and photo from Stuller, Inc.*

Advantages of electroformed jewelry

◆ It provides a big look at a relatively low price.

◆ It's lightweight and therefore ideal for earrings.

◆ It can show minute detail like one would see in a fine engraving.

Disadvantages of electroformed jewelry

◆ It dents very easily. The average thickness of the higher quality pieces is about .007", so special care is required. Electroforming would be an unsuitable process for making bracelets or rings.

◆ It cannot be repaired. Some manufacturers, however, offer a lifetime replacement warranty.

◆ It usually costs more per gram than stamped and cast jewelry. This is because expensive equipment is used to make it, and it tends to be produced in lower quantities.

♦ Even though gems have been set in electroformed jewelry, the thinness of the metal often makes setting impossible.

♦ It's usually difficult to add a textured finish to electroformed jewelry because of the thinness of the metal.

Electroformed jewelry can vary in quality depending on the manufacturer. Some pieces may have a metal thickness of only .003 of an inch. Others may lack the bright polish or stronger post assembly of a better quality piece. The thinner, more fragile pieces may be cheaper; but if they don't last as long, they shouldn't be considered a better buy.

Hand Fabrication

Hand fabrication is the oldest way of making jewelry. It involves the use of hand tools. The piece is entirely made with hand procedures such as hammering, sawing, soldering, filing, carving, setting, and finishing. Often the pieces are one-of-a-kind; but several pieces may be produced from the same design, decreasing the time and cost of fabrication.

In Europe, a higher percentage of the jewelry is hand-fabricated compared to the United States. Just as many Europeans enjoy buying bread from their local bakery, they also like the personal touch of dealing with a jeweler who makes a piece from start to finish.

Advantages of hand fabrication

♦ It requires less cleanup and finishing than casting. Therefore the backs of hand-fabricated pieces are often smoother and brighter than cast pieces.

♦ It allows exclusivity and great versatility. Each item can be unique.

♦ It shows the individuality of the craftsman.

♦ Hand-worked metal can be stronger and denser than cast metal.

♦ Hand-fabricated jewelry can be more lightweight than if it were cast, which makes it an ideal way to make comfortable earrings.

Disadvantages of hand fabrication

♦ It's usually a very time-consuming process, although in certain cases hand fabrication can be easier and faster than other methods.

Fabricating Custom Palladium Earrings

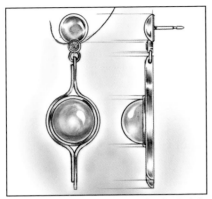

Fig. 4.15 Custom earring design by Lainie Mann with mabé pearls and pink sapphires.

Fig. 4.16 Fabricating the metal components. *Photo by Mark Mann.*

Fig. 4.17 Using graph paper to ensure identical forming. *Photo by Mark Mann.*

Fig. 4.18 Soldering the components together. *Photo by Mark Mann.*

Fig. 4.19 Finished hand-fabricated palladium earrings. *Jewelry and photo by Mark Mann.*

Fig. 4.20 Hand-fabricated gold earrings © by Ingerid Ekeland. *Photo: Oliver & Espig Jewelers.*

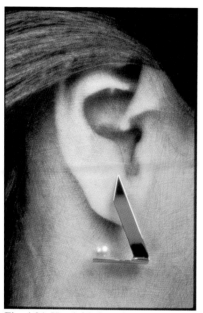

Fig. 4.21 Hand-fabricated earring of 14K gold set with a cultured pearl. *Earring and photo from Alan Revere Jewelry Design.*

Fig. 4.22 Goldsmith's signature on the back of the hand-fabricated earring in fig 4.21. *Photo by author.*

♦ It's often more expensive, because of the extra time required.

Occasionally people neglect to consider hand-crafted jewelry because they assume it will be too costly. This is a mistake. Hand-fabricated jewelry can be affordable. An example is the earring shown in figures 4.21 & 4.22. The signature of the goldsmith who designed and made it is on the back. Hand-crafted pieces like this have an important role—they offer buyers the privilege of owning a product of the creative mind rather than of a machine.

Handmade Jewelry

Within the jewelry industry, the term "handmade" has a variety of meanings and connotations. According to the Federal Trade Commission of the United States, the term "handmade" should only be applied to jewelry which is made entirely by hand methods and tools. If any part of the piece is cast or die-struck, it is not handmade. Appraisers often use this meaning for the term "handmade."

Some jewelers describe custom-made jewelry as handmade if most of the work is done by hand. They reason that a cast piece made from a hand-carved wax and then finished and set by hand can require just as much creativity and work as a hand-fabricated piece.

Chain manufacturers make a distinction between chain which is handmade and machine-made. If a rope chain, for example, is assembled by hand, it is considered handmade even if the loops have been formed by a machine.

Since "handmade" is a more generic, less precise term than "hand-fabricated," goldsmiths in America generally prefer to have their hand-crafted pieces described as "hand-fabricated" or simply "fabricated." This way it's clear that no part of the piece is cast or die-struck. To a few people, "handmade" may even sometimes have negative connotations such as "homespun" or "unsophisticated."

Since the word has so many meanings, it's best to ask salespeople and jewelers to define what they mean when they use the term "handmade"; this will prevent misunderstandings.

Why Manufacturing Methods are Often Combined

Jewelers like to take advantage of the benefits of the various manufacturing techniques. For example, the diamonds of engagement rings are often put in die-struck or hand-fabricated prong settings. Since the metal of these settings is usually harder and denser, they can hold the diamonds more securely than those which are cast. Also, the shape and thickness of the prongs is generally more consistent.

In his book, *The Retail Jeweller's Guide* (p. 200), Kenneth Blakemore mentions that it's common practice in Britain to use a cast head and hand-fabricated shank to make a gem ring. "The drawn wire (hand-fabricated) shank has more elasticity than has a cast one, and will better stand up to the stretching entailed in sizing it."

Long parallel lines or rims on an item can be of a more consistent thickness if they're hand-fabricated rather than cast. It's often better to make bracelet and necklace catches by hand so they can be an integral part of the piece.

Figure 4.23 is an example of how a jeweler can combine methods to produce a high quality piece in a cost-effective way. The scroll-like frame was cast from a hand-carved wax model. A rubber mold of it was made so the design cost could be shared by other pieces cast from it. The wire design and setting were hand-fabricated because it was easier to bend the wire than to carve a wax mold and cast and finish it. In addition, the wire patterns are cleaner and more attractive. When other scroll frames are cast from the mold, the setting and wire design can be changed to give each piece a unique look.

Fig. 4.23 An 18K white-gold brooch with cast frame and hand-crafted wirework. *Jewelry & photo from The Roxx Limited.*

Sometimes people regard cast and stamped jewelry as cheap. This is inaccurate. High-quality jewelry can be made with any of the manufacturing methods. What counts is that the jeweler is skilled and that the method(s) chosen suit the needs of the buyer and the piece.

5

Selecting the Setting

During the 2006 Tucson gem show, I purchased two blue chalcedony rings at some clearance tables (fig. 5.1). One was made of 14K white gold and the other of sterling silver. I had wanted an inexpensive pastel blue ring that I could wear when traveling without worrying about losing it. After I returned home, I decided to wear the white gold ring. Within a week, while fixing dinner, I accidentally hit the ring on the counter. The stone popped right out of its setting. Later, I decided to wear the silver ring and had a similar experience.

Even though I got a good price on the rings and they looked attractive on my hand, none of that mattered because neither of them withstood much wear. That's because the settings weren't secure. ("**Setting**" can refer to the part of a mounting that holds the gemstones or to the way the stones have been set.) Because of the low price of the rings and the type of stones set in them, I hadn't bothered to check the settings with a loupe (hand magnifier). Had I done this, it would have been obvious that the stones weren't secure. See figures 5.3–5.6. Fortunately, I didn't give the rings away as a gift; that would have been embarrassing.

To help you avoid an experience like I had, this chapter discusses the basics of selecting a secure prong setting. It also outlines the advantages and disadvantages of various setting styles so that you can choose mountings that are suited to your needs and lifestyle.

Choosing a Secure Prong (Claw) Setting

The most popular setting style for solitaire rings is the prong setting (called claw setting in the UK). This is mainly because it allows the stone to sit higher, making it appear more prominent and brilliant than it would in most other settings. The proper prong setting can hold large stones securely for years. However, some cluster prong settings are notorious for having small stones fall out of them. This is caused by the thinner prongs and the fact that often less care is taken in setting the smaller stones. As a result, a cluster setting is not the best choice for an everyday ring which will get lots of wear.

To adequately judge the quality of a setting, some type of magnifier is required. You can find 5- and 10-power hand magnifiers in coin and stamp shops and some discount stores. They sell for as little as $6 to $15 and are adequate for evaluating gold jewelry. These magnifiers can also be used for other purposes such as

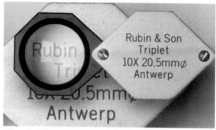

Fig. 5.1 Ten-power triplet loupe. Photo and loupe from Rubin & Son.

reading fine print or examining photo negatives. For grading gems, a 10-power triplet loupe (fig. 5.1) is usually recommended. (A triple lens structure in the loupe helps prevent distortion.) A good loupe will cost at least $25. With a little practice, you can learn to use a loupe not only for examining gems but also for checking the setting and the quality of the mounting.

Before you go shopping, it's a good idea to practice using your magnifier on some jewelry that you already own. Listed below are points you should consider when judging the quality of a prong setting.

♦ **Is there a seat for the stone in the prongs?** The seat is a cone-shaped metal band area that supports the bottom (pavilion) of a gemstone. Some people also consider the notch or groove in the prongs as part of the seat. It supports the outer circumference of the stone (the girdle). Setters use a cone-shaped drill called a bur to form the seat. Occasionally they just bend over the prongs and neglect to put in a seat. This was the problem with the chalcedony rings I purchased. There was no seat to support the base of the stone (figs. 5.3 and 5.4); thus, the gems were only held by the prongs, which had either poor grooves or no grooves. Just bending prongs over a stone will not hold it securely in place. That's why the stones in my rings got knocked out of their settings so easily. A stone without a proper seat is not secure.

Fig. 5.2 White gold and silver ring mountings with blue chalcedony stones resting on them after falling from their settings

Fig. 5.3 The walls of the circular "seat" on the silver ring are perpendicular instead of angled so they couldn't offer proper stone support.

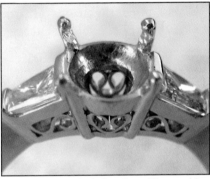

Fig. 5.4 The white gold ring does not have a proper seat either.

Fig. 5.5 Unfinished ring from Varna with a properly angled seat, which fits flush against the sloping pavilion (bottom) of a stone

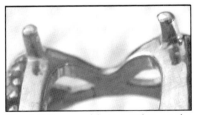
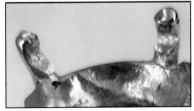

Fig. 5.6 Prongs with no notches on the 14K white gold ring

Fig. 5.7 Prongs on the Varna ring with proper notches for supporting the girdle area of the stone

All photos this page by author

♦ **Is the stone set securely in the seat?** The outside edges of the stone should be flat against the seat and the prongs should be in contact with the stone. If not, the stone won't be stable and well supported. Figures 5.3 and.5.4 are examples of improperly made seats that will not secure a stone well. You usually have to look at the setting from the side to determine if the stone is properly seated and to detect space between the prongs.

Another way to detect space between a stone and a prong is to try to slide a piece of paper between them. The paper won't pass if the prong is holding the stone properly. This test is particularly effective for checking solitaire settings.

♦ **Do the prongs look too thin or too thick?** Prongs should have enough metal to hold the stone securely but not so much that they hide its beauty. Figures 5.7 to 5.9 are examples of acceptable prongs.

♦ **Are any of the prongs or prong tips missing?** If they are, the piece may be secondhand. Otherwise, it's the result of poor casting or setting. If the prongs are missing from jewelry you own, get them repaired before a stone falls out.

♦ **Is the head soldered securely to the shank?** (The head is another term for the setting and the shank is the circular part of the ring.) Sometimes the head is attached only at a small point instead of being soldered flat against surfaces of the shank. If the joints don't fit well, they won't be as strong as they should be.

Other Setting Styles

The setting style is an important consideration when selecting mountings for fragile stones or jewelry subjected to hard wear. Some styles secure and protect stones better than others. Basic setting styles are described below with an outline of their benefits and drawbacks.

Bezel (Tube) Setting (figs. 5.10 And 5.11). This is a popular style for both men and women's jewelry. A band of metal (called a bezel) is pressed around the edge of the stone to hold it in place. The bezel protects the edge of the stone and provides a secure setting for stones subjected to a lot of wear. If I had selected blue chalcedony rings with bezel settings, I doubt the stones would have fallen out.

Fig. 5.8 Two styles of sturdy prongs on a ring with pink and white diamonds by J. Landau. *Photo by Derse Studio.*

Fig. 5.9 Another sturdy prong-setting. *Ring and photo from Varna.*

Fig. 5.10 Bezel-set emerald. *Pendant from Hubert, Inc; photo Harold & Erica Van Pelt.*

Fig. 5.11 Multiple bezel settings. *Ring and photo by Michael Sugarman*

Fig. 5.12 Partial bezel and prong setting. *Ring and photo from Varna.*

Fig. 5.13 Partial bezel setting. *Ring and photo from Varna.*

In the past, bezel settings were used mostly for cabochons (unfaceted, dome-shaped stones) such as jade and star sapphire. They are now frequently used as attractive settings for diamonds and faceted colored gemstones. The bezel may either fully or partially encircle the stone. Partial bezel settings reveal more of the stones and allow more light into them than full bezels.

Advantages of bezel setting

♦ Provides good protection for the girdle and pavilion areas of stones.

♦ Can be used to set almost all gemstones without damaging them.

♦ When done properly, holds gemstones well and doesn't require repairing and maintenance later on.

♦ Accentuates the circumference of the stone, making it appear larger than in prong setting.

♦ Provides a smooth ring surface, which does not snag clothing.

Disadvantage of bezel setting:

♦ Usually more time consuming and expensive than prong and bead setting.

Channel Setting (figs. 5.14 & 5.16). This style is often used for bands, but it may also be used to accent center stones. The gemstones are suspended in a channel of vertical walls with no metal separating them.

Advantages of channel setting

♦ Protects the girdle area of the diamonds.

♦ Provides a smooth ring surface.

♦ Is appropriate for enhancing ring shanks and for creating linear designs with a tailored look.

Disadvantages of channel setting

♦ Risky, in terms of damage to stones during setting, so it should not be used for fragile gems.

Fig. 5.14 Channel-set raw and princess-cut diamonds. *Ring by Todd Reed, photo by azadphoto.com.*

Fig. 5.15 Bar setting. *Diamond ring and photo from Stuller, Inc.*

Fig. 5.16 Channel setting. *Amethyst ring and photo from Stuller, Inc.*

Fig. 5.17 Bar-set rubies and bead-set diamonds. *Ring and photo from Stuller, Inc.*

Fig. 5.18 Pavé-set citrines. *Earrings and photo from Stuller, Inc.*

Fig. 5.19 Pavé-set shank, bead-set prongs and prong-set brown diamond. *Ring and photo from King Plutarco, Inc.*

63

♦ Usually channel setting is more time consuming and costly than prong setting, when properly done. Some channel setting is done cheaply and quickly by simply cutting a long groove in thin metal and sliding diamonds in, but the stones may not be secure. In good channel setting, the stones are placed individually in seats in a sturdy channel with sufficient metal along both sides of the channel to support them well.

Bar Setting (figs. 5.15 and 5.17). This is a form of channel setting, except the stones are set in channels across a ring, and the stones on each end of the channel are exposed at the edges of the mounting instead of being secured in metal. As a result, the bar-set stones can get loose or chipped with repeated banging. Channel setting is more secure because the channel is enclosed with metal at each end. Otherwise, bar setting has the same advantages as channel setting.

Bead or pavé setting (figs. 5.17 to 5.19). In this type of setting, gemstones are fit into tapered holes and set almost level with the surface of the ring. Then some of the surrounding metal is raised to form beads which hold the stones in place. This style is frequently used for women's jewelry. Sometimes the metal around the bead-set stones is raised or engraved to form decorative patterns.

When there are three or more rows of gemstones set in this way without partitions between the stones, it is called **pavé**, which, in French, means "paved" like a cobblestone road (fig. 5.18). The jewelry trade often refers to any type of bead setting as pavé. In order to give the impression of a continuous diamond surface, it is customary to use white gold or platinum to support pavé-set diamonds even if the rest of the mounting is yellow gold. Rhodium plating is sometimes added to further heighten this effect.

Advantages of bead or pavé setting:

♦ Usually protects gemstones better than prong setting.

♦ Allows uninterrupted designs of varying width. When pavé designs are spread over the surface of a mounting, they can make gemstones appear larger and more numerous than they actually are.

Fig. 5.21 Invisible-set rubies and bead-set diamonds. *Ring & photo from Stuller, Inc.*

Fig. 5.20 Flush-set diamonds. *Ring and photo from Mark Schneider.*

Disadvantages of bead or pavé setting:

♦ Is a risky setting method in terms of possible stone damage. Good diamonds, rubies, and sapphires can withstand the pressure of being pavé set, but fragile stones such as emeralds, opals, tourmalines and diamonds with large cracks risk damage.

♦ Doesn't provide as smooth of a ring surface as bezel, channel and flush setting.

♦ May not be as secure as other settings.

Flush Setting (fig. 5.20). Flush setting is a popular style for people who use their hands a lot in their professions; it offers good protection for their diamonds. The stone is fit snugly into a tapered hole that is grooved to hold the girdle of the stone. Then the surrounding metal is pressed and hammered around the rim of the opening to secure the gemstone.

Advantages of flush setting

♦ Protects the girdle area of diamonds.

♦ When done properly, holds diamonds well.

♦ Provides a smooth, tailored look.

Disadvantages of flush setting

♦ Is usually more time consuming and expensive than prong and bead setting.

♦ Is a very risky setting method, in terms of damage to stones, so it should not be used for fragile gems.

Invisible setting (fig. 5.21). Invisible-set gemstones are placed tightly next to each other with the metal of the setting concealed underneath the stones, allowing them to form a continuous surface.

Advantages of invisible setting

♦ Emphasizes the diamonds more than other styles since the metal setting is concealed.

♦ Enhances brilliance because there's no metal on the top of the stone to impede the entry of light.

♦ Allows jewelry designers to create a smooth, uninterrupted gemstone surface with square stones.

Disadvantages of invisible setting

♦ It costs more than most other setting styles because it requires expensive machinery and highly skilled setters.

♦ If not properly set, small square stones may fall out with hard wear.

♦ Not many setters know how to do and repair invisible setting, particularly with round stones. **Make sure that the store who sells you invisibly-set jewelry will service it for you**.

It's not common practice for jewelry customers to analyze which setting styles would be best for their needs and why, but it should be. Too often, jewelry that looks attractive when bought turns out to be impractical. With a bit of forethought, it's possible to select a style that is not only aesthetically pleasing but functional as well. However, no matter how suitable the style, if a stone is not properly set, there could be durability problems. To avoid them, deal with jewelers who place an importance on good craftsmanship.

6

Finishes & Decorative Techniques

One of the most effective ways for jewelers to create variety and interest in their pieces is to texturize or decorate the metal. This also has practical benefits. Textured surfaces are less likely to show scratches, nicks and other signs of wear than surfaces with a high polish. This chapter outlines and illustrates traditional finishes and decorative techniques. They are often combined to create distinctive jewelry.

Finishes

Bright polish   Mirror-like, **shiny finish** (fig. 6.1). It may also be called a **high polish**.

Brushed finish   Tiny parallel lines are scratched on the surface with a wire brush creating soft, diffused reflections. The effect created depends on the size of the lines. A coarsely brushed finish may suggest a strong masculine quality (fig. 6.2).

Florentine finish   An engraved series of cross-hatched patterns with coarser lines than a brushed finish.

Glassbeaded finish   A matte finish achieved by blasting metal with minute glass beads using a sandblasting machine. Part of the surface of the pendant in figure 6.5 has a glassbeaded finish. Fingerprints on this glass-beaded surface won't show. If it had been blasted with sand, the finish would be coarser and would tend to darken from skin oil. Some jewelers resolve this problem with sandblasted finishes by touching the whole sandblasted area with their fingers to give it a uniform color.

Fig. 6.1 Bright polish. *Ring and photo from Mark Schneider.*

Fig. 6.2 Coarse brushed finish. *Rings and photo from Aaron Henry Design Goldsmith.*

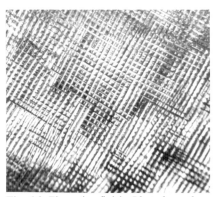

Fig. 6.3 Florentine finish. *Photo by author.*

Fig. 6.4 Florentine finish. *Ring and photo from True Knots Wedding Band Co.*

Fig. 6.5 Glassbeaded finish on a pendant designed by Peggy Croft. *Photo by author.*

Fig. 6.6 Hammered finish. *Ring and photo from True Knots Wedding Band Co.*

Hammered finish   As the name suggests, the finish is created by multiple hammer marks on the surface (figs. 6.6 & 6.11). The appearance varies depending on the size and type of hammer used.

Matte finish   A dull, non-reflective finish. Brushed, satin, and glassbeaded finishes can be classified as matte. Matte finishes help emphasize the color of the metal and create subdued looks. They also diminish or eliminate reflections. When shiny and matte finishes are juxtaposed, interesting designs can be created.

I've found another use for matte finishes—to make gold crowns on teeth less noticeable. A gold crown on one of my molars would catch the light and was especially noticeable when I smiled. I asked my dentist to put a matte finish on the crown and the problem was corrected.

Sandblasted finish   A matte finish made by blasting metal with sand (figs. 6.8 & 6.9). It's grainier than a glassbeaded finish. Some people in the trade may use the term "sandblasted" to also mean "glassbeaded" since both finishes are produced by a sandblasting machine.

Satin finish   A very finely brushed surface texture resembling satin (fig 6.10). This finish can add a soft refined touch to the piece.

Decorative Techniques

Anticlastic Raising   A metal-forming process in which the center of a flat metal sheet is compressed while its edges are stretched. The resulting form resembles a saddle and has two curves at right angles to each other moving in opposite directions (fig. 6.12).

Fig. 6.7 Matte finish. *Ring and photo from The Bell Group Rio Grande.*

Fig. 6.8 Sandblasted & shiny finish. *Ring & photo by True Knots Wedding Band Co.*

Fig. 6.9 Fine sandblasted finish. *Ring and photo from True Knots Wedding Band Co.*

Fig. 6.10 Satin finish. *Ring and photo from True Knots Wedding Band Co.*

Fig. 6.11 Fine hammered finish. *Pendant by Gary Dulac, photo by John Parrish.*

Fig. 6.12 Anticlastic raising and twisting. *Earring copyright by Ingerid Ekeland; photo from Oliver & Espig jewelers.*

The opposite process is **synclastic**, whereby a flat sheet is shaped by compressing its edges and stretching its center. This creates a form which has curves all moving in the same direction as in a conventional bowl.

Braiding

Technically, an ornamental pattern that is a braid (fig 6.13). The term is also used loosely to describe border patterns made by twisting wires and soldering or fusing them to the edge of a jewelry piece (fig. 6.14).

Chasing

A technique of indenting and depressing a relief design into metal from the front using chisels and punches. No metal is lost during the process.

Chiseling

Same technique as chasing except some of the metal is removed.

Embossing

A technique of creating a raised design by pushing metal out from its reverse side with hammers and punches. The process can also be done mechanically using dies.

Enameling

Fusion of a colored glass onto metal to create a design. One technique in which thin flattened wire partitions (called cloisons) are filled with enamel is called **cloisonné** (fig 6.15). *Cloison* is French for "partition." This process of decorating metal was used extensively in Western Europe during the Byzantine Era and the Middle Ages. It's still popular in Japan and China.

Engraving

A line design cut into metal. Most engraving today is done by machine, but skilled hand engravers are still in demand. Figures 6.16, 6.23 and 6.24 are examples of hand engraving.

Etching

A process of using acids and a resist such as varnish to create a design on metal by corrosion.

Filigree

A delicate, lacelike design often made by bending and soldering fine wires (fig. 6.17).

Fig. 6.13 Braiding. Bracelet by Henry Dunay from *Joseph DuMouchelle Auctioneers; photo by David Behl.*

Fig. 6.14 Gold braiding and platinum embossing. *Ring from Gelin & Abaci.*

Fig. 6.15 Cloisonné enameling

Fig. 6.16 A hand engraving. *Photo from the engraver, Hans Kober.*

Fig. 6.17 Filigree pendant from Divina Pearls. *Photo by Cristina Gregory.*

Fig. 6.18 Granulation. *Pendant by Zaffiro; photo by Daniel Van Rossen.*

Steps to Making an Engraved Palladium Ring

Fig. 6.19 Wax model of ring for the casting process. *Wax model and photo by Mark Mann.*

Fig. 6.20 Finished rough casting. *Ring and photo by Mark Mann.*

Fig. 6.21 Relief engraving of polished ring. *Engraving and photo by Steece Hermanson.*

Fig. 6.22 Application of a fine stipple finish to the recessed portion by Steece Hermanson. *Photo by Steece Hermanson.*

Fig. 6.23 Finished engraved palladium ring. *Ring and photo by Mark Mann.*

Fig. 6.24 Decorative engraving on a Varna platinum ring. *Photo from Varna.*

Fig. 6.25 Note the natural-looking coloring of the migrant fieldfare (thrush) on this 9K gold brooch. The orange, brown, and black colors were created by heating the gold until it turned black through oxidation. Later, the craftsman artfully worked down the metal to expose the gradations of color. *Photo by the designer, Alan Hodgkinson.*

Fusion

Melting metal to produce interesting forms and textures. It also refers to the process of uniting two metals using heat and no solder.

Granulation

Tiny metal balls fused to a metal base. No solder is used. This is an ancient technique which enabled the Etruscans to achieve the look of a large quantity of gold when it was in short supply. They organized gold granules as small as 1/200th of an inch thick onto thin sheets of gold and then attached them using heat.

Milgraining

A beaded line pattern made by hand or machine (figs. 6.26 & 6.28). It's often used as an ornamental border on the edges of wedding bands.

Mokume gane

An ancient Japanese technique of making wood-grain patterns using layers of contrasting colored metals such as copper and steel or yellow gold and palladium (fig. 6.31). Mokume gane, which means "wood-grain metal" in Japanese, was first used to decorate samurai swords.

Oxidizing

A process of darkening or coloring a metal surface through oxidation. For example, a flame with oxygen can produce a dark antique-like surface finish on low-karat gold alloys.

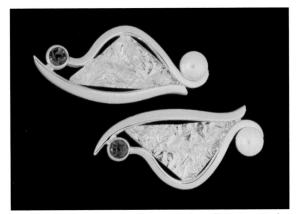

Fig. 6.26 Milgraining on a marquis chain

Fig. 6.27 Reticulation. *Earrings and photo from Gary Dulac Goldsmith.*

Fig. 6.28 Milgraining. *Paraiba tourma-line ring and photo from Hubert Inc.*

Fig. 6.29 Stippled gold earrings by Konstantina Mahlia. *Photo Robin Stancliff.*

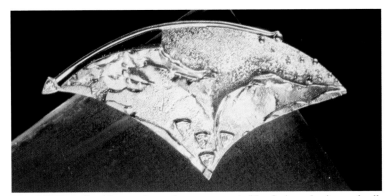

Fig. 6.30 Brooch with granules and textures created by fusion, chasing and roll printing. *Photo from the designer and craftsman, Richard Kimball.*

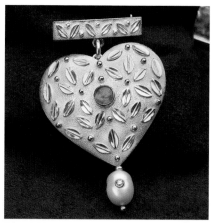

Fig. 6.32 Contrasting polished gold laurel-leaf motifs and granulation on a gold background with a stipple finish. *Pendant by Konstantina Mahlia, copyright by the Mahlia Collection; photo by Robin Stancliff*

Fig. 6.31 Mokume gane 14K yellow, red, green and gray gold rings with etched copper and silver by George Sawyer. *Photo by Peter Lee.*

Pebbled texture	A pebble-like appearance achieved by hammering the metal.
Repoussé	The process of raising a design in sheet metal by punching up the back side. Repoussé is then finished from the front by chasing.
Reticulation	A texturing technique which involves a controlled, localized melting of the surface, causing it to texturize into ridges and valleys. The deeper underlying metal remains unchanged (fig. 6.27).
Roller printing	A technique that transfers a texture from one material to another. A "sandwich" made of two sheets of metal and a texturing material such as fabric, lace, tough plant materials or screen is passed between them through a rolling mill under pressure. Both pieces are embossed with the reverse image of the material.
Stamping	Impressing shapes, patterns or textures with hardened steel tools called punches.
Stippling	Indentation or hammering of metal using a pointed tool (figs. 6.22, 6.29, & 6.32).

Judging Finish

Many jewelers feel that one of the easiest ways for the lay person to judge craftsmanship is to look at the back of the jewelry piece. If it's well-finished on the back and underneath, chances are it's well constructed. Look at figure 6.33 and note the roughness of the metal. Further examination reveals a lot of porosity, irregular prongs, poorly soldered joints and excess solder.

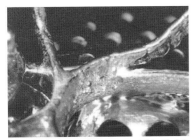

Fig. 6.33 A rough, unacceptable finish

Fig. 6.34 Cast ring with an average

Figs. 6.35 & 6.36 Front and back of a cast 18K gold brooch custom-designed for the amethysts. Note the attractive finish. *Brooch and photos from Forest Jewelers.*

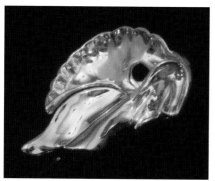 

Fig. 6.37 A high-quality finish on the back of the cast brooch in fig. 6.5. *Photo by author.*

Fig. 6.38 Enamel on the inside of a bracelet. *Jewelry & photo from Tempus Gems.*

Figure 6.34 is an example of a piece with an average finish. It's not easy to polish the inner curved surfaces of cast jewelry. Even though the interior of this ring is not perfectly smooth, the company that made it eliminated the roughness, making it an acceptable mounting. The ring also feels comfortable when worn.

Now look at the back of the cast brooch in figure 6.37. It took about one hour to clean and prepare it for polishing after casting. Then another four to five hours were spent polishing it to give it the smooth and shiny inner surface. Knowing how much work is required to craft a piece well makes it easier to understand jewelry pricing. The front of the brooch is shown at the beginning of this chapter in figure 6.5 as an example of a glassbeaded finish. The back is a good example of a shiny finish.

Figures 6.35 and 6.36 show the front and back of a well-polished brooch. Not only is it cleanly finished, it has an attractive decorative design. The fact that the jeweler could make the back of this piece look as good as the front indicates he has the skill and desire to construct it properly too. Figure 6.38 is another example a jewelry piece that is as attractive on the inside as it is on the outside. In this case, enameling was used to decorate the inside.

The feel of a jewelry piece is a good indication of the quality of its finish and polish. If the piece has jagged edges, file marks or sharp points that scratch you or catch on your clothing, it's not well finished. High-quality pieces will have a smooth, polished finish throughout, even in the areas behind the gemstones. When evaluating jewelry, check the back of the piece. But expect to pay more when a jeweler has spent considerable time creating a piece that is equally attractive on the back, inside and front.

7

Choosing Flattering Jewelry

When chosen wisely, jewelry can enhance your appearance and draw attention to features you wish to emphasize. In this chapter, you'll learn basic principles that can help you achieve your desired look. Four factors you should consider when selecting jewelry for yourself or as a gift for others are:

♦ Proportions or scale
♦ Linear direction
♦ Repetition
♦ Coordination with clothing and accessories

To understand how you can use these elements to create favorable or unfavorable illusions with your jewelry, you should be familiar with basic face and neck types. Five typical face shapes are:

① OVAL   ③ HEART   ⑤ SQUARE   ② LONG / RECTANGLE   ④ ROUND

Diagrams by Bonnie Nelson

Four neck types are:

OVAL / SHORT-NECK   OVAL / LONG NECK

OVAL / WIDE NECK

OVAL / SLENDER NECK

Diagrams by Bonnie Nelson

Keep in mind that the categories above are not absolute. Fashion designers differ in the way they describe the shapes and sizes of people and the parts of their body.

Overall body size also plays a role in how jewelry looks on a person, but this book focuses on the areas of the body where jewelry is most often worn and describes body types in general terms such as tall and short. Otherwise the discussion would be too involved and confusing. Let's look at the four design elements one by one:

Proportions or scale: This refers to the size of a jewelry piece in relation to your body. As a general rule, jewelry is most flattering when it is in proportion to your height and build. Large or tall people tend to look best in average to bold-sized jewelry; tiny jewelry could go unnoticed. On the other hand, huge jewelry pieces on petite people may look distracting or out of harmony with their build. This doesn't mean that petite people should never wear bold jewelry. It only means that small- to average-size jewelry will probably be more complementary and more suitable for a wider variety of occasions.

Linear Direction: Jewelry can have line elements that direct the viewer's eye to move in a desired direction. These lines allow you to create the illusion of being thinner or broader, or taller or shorter. For example, a v-neck shaped necklace with a long vertical pendant can make a person's face and body appear thinner and longer. The three basic line directions are vertical, horizontal and diagonal. They have the following effects:

♦ **Vertical lines**: They slim and elongate, creating a strong vertical line, and they suggest strength and alertness like someone who is upright.

♦ **Horizontal lines:** They broaden and shorten, and they may suggest calmness and restfulness like someone lying down.

♦ **Diagonal lines:** They slim and elongate and suggest dynamic action.

The predominant line of a piece can either be part of the design or part of the overall silhouette or outline of a piece. Lines can also be used to direct the eye to desirable features of a person's body or clothing.

Repetition: This refers to the reuse of shapes, patterns, colors and styles. Repetition accentuates features. For example square earrings emphasize a square face, whereas round or oval earrings would de-emphasize the squareness. As a general rule, do not repeat an element that you do not wish to emphasize.

Coordination with clothing and accessories. Ideal jewelry choices not only depend on a person's features and body shape, but on the clothes they wear with the jewelry. For example, you should consider the neckline of a dress or blouse when determining a suitable necklace to wear with it. In most cases, the necklace should fall above or below the neckline, not at the neckline. A halter top or frilly collar may look best with no necklace. Patterned clothes may require plain or simple jewelry, whereas basic single-color clothing may look stunning with elaborate jewelry.

Color should also be considered. Usually the color of your jewelry should go with what you wear and should complement your complexion, but there are exceptions. Even though some fashion writers say it's best, for example, to wear silver, platinum and white gold with cool-toned skin and yellow-gold with warm-toned skin, I don't think it matters which color metal you wear as long as you like it. For centuries, kings, queens, dignitaries and movie stars with cool-toned skin have worn flattering yellow-gold jewelry. They have also combined it with platinum jewelry and even silver jewelry. Prestigious designers now incorporate different metals and metal colors into their designs. So you needn't be concerned if the metal in your wedding ring doesn't match your other jewelry.

The following chapters provide more detailed tips on selecting jewelry that will complement your face, neck, hands and wrists. My goal is not to dictate what you should wear, but to help you select flattering jewelry that will meet your needs. The right jewelry is the type that makes you look and feel your best.

8

Selecting Necklaces

The necklace may have been born more than 100,000 years ago. The June 23, 2006 issue of *Science* magazine reported that three bead-like shells from ancient Israel and Algeria came from the same layer of soil where archaeologists found human remains dating to between 100,000 and 135,000 years ago. In April 2004, a group of scientists excavating a cave in South Africa discovered 41 mollusk shells that appeared to have been strung as necklace beads about 75,000 years ago. Bones, stones and teeth were also used for ancient jewelry. Gold may have first appeared in necklaces around 2500 BC.

In some cultures, necklaces evolved into being a sign of high office and achievement. They were worn by kings and people of high status. Even today, necklaces are used to honor Olympic champions and the bravest soldiers. They are also part of the ceremonial ornaments of priests of some religions. Nowadays necklaces are a common jewelry item worn primarily by females. However, chain necklaces are becoming increasingly popular with males.

This chapter outlines the various types of necklaces available and their typical lengths, and it provides practical tips on selecting them.

Necklace Lengths and Styles

The jewelry trade has specific names for different necklace lengths. Some are as follows:

1. **Choker:** A 14–16 inch (35–40 cm) necklace that normally descends to the hollow of the throat or just below it.

Courtesy Mikimoto Co.

2. **Princess**: A 16–20 inch (40–50 cm) necklace.

3. **Matinee**: A 20–26 inch (50–66 cm) necklace. Some people like to wear a matinee length along with a choker.

4. **Opera**: A necklace about twice the size of a choker.

5. **Rope**: Necklace longer than an opera length. The defined length will vary according to the jeweler or company using the term.

   Pearl necklace lengths are summarized in the following table:

Type of necklace	Length in inches	Metric length
Choker	14–16"	35–40 cm
Princess	16–20"	40–50 cm
Matinee	20–26"	50–66 cm
Opera	28–36"	70–90 cm
Rope	40" +x	1 meter and higher

Other terms are also used to describe necklaces. These include:

Bib: A necklace of three or more concentric strands. The lowest strand normally does not fall below a matinee length.

Dog collar: A multi-strand choker-length necklace, which is also referred to as simply a collar necklace. The strands may be clasped together in a single clasp. "Dog collars" help conceal neck wrinkles.

Lariat: A cord, chain or strand of pearls or beads about 35"–60" long, which usually has a bead, pearl, pendant or tassel at both ends. No clasp is needed; it can tie or loop in front, and the ends of the necklace dangle like a necktie. Lariats can be worn a variety of ways, even as a belt.

Riviere: A **straight-line necklace** of varying length made solely of gemstones, typically diamonds. It resembles a tennis bracelet.

Sautoir: A necklace similar in length to a rope necklace and often adorned with a pendant or tassel.

Collar necklace

Long matinee necklace

Short lariat necklace

The pearl necklaces are from A & Z pearls and have oyster clasps, a hinged clasp, which allows versatility. See Chapter 14 for more necklace styles. *Photos by Diamond Graphics*

Fig 8.4 A lariat modeled by the designer of the necklace, Konstantina Mahlia. *Necklace from the Mahlia Collection; photo by Richard Petrillo.*

Fig 8.5 Close-up view of a riviere (straight-line) diamond necklace from Abe Mor Diamond Cutters & Co. *Photo by KD Imaging.*

Station necklace: a chain with a design element such as a gemstone or pearl that occurs at regular intervals along the necklace. One example is the **"tin cup"** pearl necklace, which has short lengths of chain alternating with a pearl.

Torsade: A multi-strand necklace formed by twisting strands around each other (fig. 8.6).

Uniform strand: A strand whose pearls or beads are all about the same size.

Graduated strand: A strand with pearls or beads of different sizes which gradually get larger towards the center. Graduated pearl strands can provide a big pearl look at a lower price than uniform strands.

Fancy necklace: A necklace that doesn't fit neatly into the preceding categories. The term "fancy" is also used as a category name for unusual gems shapes, colors or chains. The necklace in figure 8.6 is an example of a fancy necklace. It isn't a typical collar or choker necklace. Consequently, it might be described as a fancy collar necklace.

Selecting Flattering Necklaces

Chapter 7 discussed three types of lines and described the illusions they can create as follows:

♦ **Vertical lines**: They slim and elongate.

♦ **Horizontal lines:** They broaden and shorten.

♦ **Diagonal lines:** They slim and elongate

Based on these principles, which of the preceding necklace styles do you think would most likely make the face appear broader?

Answer: The dog collar or any choker-length necklace style is ideal if you want your face or neck to appear broader or shorter because they encourage your eye to move horizontally across the neck instead of up and down your body. If you wish to de-emphasize a long neck, there is one type of choker that may have the opposite effect, and that's a very large multi-strand choker. It could have the effect of accentuating the neck. If you wish to wear a choker without emphasizing a short neck and broad face, consider adding a long pendant to the choker, or choose a thin, delicate choker.

Fig 8.6 Sardinian coral torsade with a hand-carved shell cameo clasp. *Necklace by Zaffiro; photo by Daniel Van Rossen.*

Fig 8.7 A "tin cup" Tahitian cultured pearl necklace—station necklace from A & Z pearls. *Photo by Diamond Graphics.*

Fig 8.8 A fancy collar necklace set with cultured pearls and colored gemstones. *Necklace from King Plutarco, Inc; photo by Diamond Graphics.*

Since vertical and diagonal lines can have a slimming effect, long strands, v-neck shaped necklaces and chains with long pendants can be good choices if you want to slenderize and lengthen your face, neck and body. They are especially flattering to people with round or square faces, but no matter what your face shape you can still look good in long necklaces depending on the style.

Repetition of shapes tends to draw attention to the shape. Therefore, if you wish to de-emphasize a square or rectangular face or angular features, select a round, oval or curved shaped necklace and/or pendant.

When selecting a necklace to wear with an outfit, pay attention to where it falls in relation to the neckline of the outfit. Jet Taylor, a bridal

consultant in Charlotte, North Carolina recommends that brides wear their pearl necklace at least one inch above the neckline so it will not look as if it is going to fall into the dress. If the necklace is longer, it should be at least two inches below the neckline so that it will show and the necklace cannot fall into the dress. This advice also applies to other types of necklaces.

If you want to de-emphasize a large stomach or bust, wear necklaces above the bust. Long necklaces can draw attention to these areas. A small bustline, however, can be an ideal place for bold neck pieces.

Proportion also plays a role in the selection of a necklace. Large and wide necklaces and chains are normally not the best choice for petite people. Yet they can be quite flattering on people who are tall. A general rule of thumb is to select jewelry that's proportionate with your body. However, there are exceptions. Oversized beads on a full-figured woman, for example, may accentuate her large build.

The best way to find out if a necklace is flattering is to try it on and look at yourself in a full length mirror. Get comments, too, from people with a good eye for style. Don't worry about the current fad. It's more important to wear a piece that enhances your appearance.

9

Chains and Other Neckwear

The previous chapter discussed some aesthetic aspects of necklace selection. This chapter deals more with practical considerations, and focuses on chains and clasps. There are several basic types of chains and they may be solid or hollow:

♦ Rope

♦ Flat chain: e.g., herringbone, omega, serpentine

♦ Link chain: e.g., cable, curb, box, figaro, Singapore, mesh

♦ Fancy chain: e.g., San Marco, kisses and hugs

♦ Snake chain

♦ Bead chain

Fig. 9.1 Rope chain

Fig. 9.2 Herringbone (flat) chain

Fig 9.3 Link chain

Fig. 9.4 San Marco (fancy) chain

Fig 9.5 Snake chain. *Photo Stuller. Inc.*

Fig. 9.6 Bead chain. *Photo from Stuller, Inc.*

Chain Lengths

The sizes of chains are more standardized than other types of necklaces. The table below lists standard lengths for chains in the USA and in metric countries.

Table 9.1 Standard chain lengths

Length in inches	Metric length
16"	40 cm
18"	45 cm
20"	50 cm
24"	60 cm
30"	75 cm
36"	90 cm

Advantages and Drawbacks of Various Chains

Rope Chain

Rope chain, like some other types of chain, can be solid or hollow (fig 9.7). It can also be machine made or hand made. Each type has advantages and drawbacks.

Advantages of solid rope chain

♦ It's ideal for suspending pendants and charms. However, the heavier the pendant, the thicker the chain should be. Good salespeople will be able to help you select a chain of an appropriate thickness if you show them the type of pendant(s) you plan to wear on the chain.

Fig 9.7 Top: hollow rope chain, bottom: solid rope chain. *Photo by author.*

♦ Solid rope chain is sturdy, especially compared to hollow rope chain and flat chains like the herringbone. The thicker the chain, the stronger it is.

♦ In some countries such as the United States, its price per gram may be a little less than other types of chain. This is because much of it may be produced domestically and has no import duties levied on it.

Disadvantage of solid rope chain

♦ Even though it can be repaired to look like new, it's not as easy to repair as a solid link chain. Hand-made rope, however, is easier to repair than the machine-made type.

Advantages of hollow rope chain

♦ It's lighter in weight than solid chain and thus more comfortable.

♦ It costs about half the price of solid chain of the same width.

Disadvantages of hollow rope chain

♦ Even though it can be repaired, it may not look like new afterwards. If there's a hole or break at one point of the chain, there is likely to be a weakness elsewhere. Repairs can become a never-ending process with hollow chains of any style.

♦ It's not a good chain for suspending heavy pendants or charms. The friction of the pendant wears down the thin metal wall, and the chain breaks. Some hollow chains come with a lifetime guarantee, but the guarantee does not cover loss or damage to a pendant when the chain breaks. If the receipt is lost or misplaced, the guarantee may not be valid.

♦ It's not a good choice for a bracelet. The banging and knocks that occur on the wrist can dent the chain.

♦ Its price per gram is usually a bit higher than solid rope.

Salespeople are supposed to tell you if a chain is hollow. Some, however, may be unaware of the hollow center or else afraid of losing the sale if they disclose this. A lightweight feel or advertising terms such as "semi-solid" and "50% lighter" are signals that a chain is hollow.

Diamond-Cut Rope

Note the tiny flat surfaces on the upper chain in figure 9.8. These reflect light like the facets of a gemstone and give the chain a brighter look. The process of cutting these surfaces is called **diamond cutting**. Since diamond-cut rope sparkles more than standard rope, it tends to sell better.

Fig. 9.8 Top: diamond-cut rope, bottom: standard rope. *Photo by author.*

Some customers complain that diamond-cut rope snags their clothes while other are pleased with it. The difference in satisfaction most likely depends on the manufacturing process. Some manufacturers do a poor finishing job and leave rough surfaces, whereas others give it a high-quality finish. Part of the problem may be the use of old instead of new diamonds to cut the facets. When buying diamond-cut rope, brush it against your clothing and run it lightly through your fingers to see if it snags or scratches. This will help determine if it's well-finished or not.

Handmade Rope

Considering its complexity, handmade rope is relatively inexpensive. In fact, in the United States, some high-quality domestic hand-made rope may sell for a bit less per gram than some Italian machine-made rope. It only takes about an hour for a skilled rope maker to assemble links into an 18", 3mm rope (It takes twice as long to make an 18" inch 1mm rope). Additional time is required to solder and finish the rope.

Fig. 9.9 Two handmade ropes magnified. The upper one is more tightly assembled and therefore stronger. *Photo by author.*

There are various qualities of handmade rope. A high-quality 14K rope will have:

♦ a flexible, tight weave, giving it strength

♦ a smooth, well-finished surface

♦ links of 14K plumb gold (not 13K or 13.5K)

♦ 14K solder instead of a low-karat solder

A good way to compare the weave is to twist the rope slightly. A loosely assembled rope will untwist to a longer length than one which is tighter.

Flat Chain

One of the most popular flat chains on the market is the herringbone (figs 9.10 and 9.11). Some jewelers, however, won't stock it because it kinks so easily (fig 9.12).

Fig 9.10 Herringbone chain. *Photos: author.*

Fig. 9.11 Patterned herringbone chain.

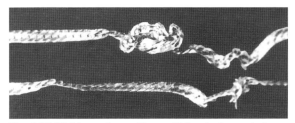

Fig. 9.12 Kinking—the problem with herringbone chain.

Advantages of herringbone chain

♦ It offers a big look at a low price. The flatness of the chain makes it wider than other types of chain of the same weight and price.

♦ It often looks shinier than rope and link chain. This is because of the light reflecting off a broader surface area.

♦ It's available in a wide variety of styles and finishes.

Disadvantages of herringbone chain

♦ It's not durable (fig. 9.12). Generally, the more lightweight it is, the more likely it is to kink or break. Some of the more flexible or heavier styles may be less likely to kink.

♦ It's not a good chain for pendants.

♦ It's difficult to repair properly. The mended part may be rigid.

When interviewing jewelers and chain dealers for this book, the author did not find one who recommended herringbone chains. The overall consensus was, "Why buy a herringbone chain when there are so many better ones to choose from?"

In general, flat chains don't last as long as solid link and rope chains, and repairing them may be a problem. Some of the thicker ones such as the **omega** (fig. 9.13) do wear better than the herringbone. Several jewelers mentioned that the **serpentine (s-chain)** has a tendency to kink. In fairness to the serpentine chain, the one in figure 9.14 has been worn by the owner day and night for many years and is still in good condition. As with any chain, the thickness has a lot to do with its durability.

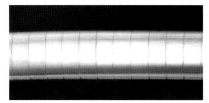 

Fig. 9-13 Omega chain. *Photos: author*   **Fig. 9-14** Serpentine or S-chain

Link Chain

Solid-link chains get the highest ratings for durability from jewelers and chain dealers alike. Link chains come in a variety of sizes—from the small, basic ring-in-ring **cable chain** (fig. 9.15) to striking jumbo necklaces and bracelets. Cable chain is commonly used for small pendants. Normally the thicker the link, the stronger it is, provided it's solid and well-soldered. A link chain that has been twisted about 85° and then flattened is often called a **curb link** (fig 9.16).

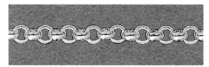 

Fig 9.15 Cable chain. *Chain & photo from H. S. Walsh & Sons Ltd.*   **Fig. 9.16** Curb link chain. *Chain & photo from H. S. Walsh & Sons Ltd..*

Link chains come in a wide variety of styles and they may be solid or hollow. One link chain that's particularly popular is the **anchor chain** (fig. 9.17). Verbally,

Fig. 9.17 Flat anchor chain. *Photo by author.*

it's often referred to as the **Gucci chain**, but this an infringement of the Gucci trademark. Another popular link chain is the **figaro**. It usually has an alternating pattern of one large and three small links (it can also have patterns of 1-2, 1-4, etc.). Sometimes the alternating pattern is combined with other chain styles (fig. 9.18).

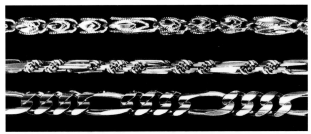

Fig. 9.18 Top—figaro marquis, center—figarope, bottom—figaro

A variation of the curb link chain is the **Singapore chain**. This is one of the strongest lightweight chains on the market. Naturally, though, the thinner the chain, the more susceptible it is

Fig. 9.19 Singapore chain. *Photo by author.*

to breaking. A close-up view (fig 9.19) shows that the Singapore chain is essentially a twisted double curb-link chain.

If the links of chain are rectangular and resemble a line of little boxes when connected, the chain is called **box chain** (fig. 9.20). Most of the

box chain on the market is relatively small and lightweight. It's
most frequently used for hanging
charms and small pendants. Naturally, the thicker the box link is,
the stronger the chain will be.

Fig. 9.20 Box chain & photo: Stuller, Inc.

Because it's made up of flat surfaces that reflect light, box chain may
look brighter than some other small chains. Another advantage is that it
doesn't knot as easily as some cable chain. It can also be repaired. Box
chain can break if it's very thin, and some of it does not allow pendants
to roll as easily as a rope or cable chain.

Thin links of chain that are interconnected lengthwise and width wise
can form **mesh chain** (fig. 9.21).

If two or more link chains are *soldered* parallel next to each other,
they may form what is called **Bismarck chain** (fig. 9.22).

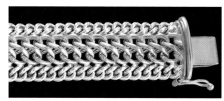
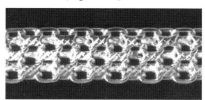

Fig. 9.21 Mesh chain & photo: Stuller, Inc.   **Fig. 9.22** Bismarck chain. *Photo: author.*

Advantages of *solid* link chain

♦ It's normally strong, but the thicker the links, the stronger the chain.

♦ It's generally a good chain for pendants. Some styles are more suited
to this than others.

♦ It's usually easy to repair to its original state.

♦ It's normally flexible and hangs nicely.

Disadvantages of solid link chain

♦ It generally costs more than hollow chains and herringbone chain of
the same width because it weighs more.

♦ It's usually not as flashy as hollow chains and herringbone chains of
the same weight.

Disadvantages of hollow link chain

♦ It's hard and sometimes impossible to repair.

♦ It's not a good chain for suspending heavy pendants. The friction of the pendant wears down the thin metal wall, and the chain breaks

♦ It's not a good choice for a bracelet. The banging and knocks that occur on the wrist can dent the chain.

Fancy Chain

Unusual chains that look like bracelets and necklaces are often referred to as **fancy chains**. The die-striking (stamping) process by which they are frequently made results in a bright polish. Three examples of fancy chains are the **San Marco** (fig. 9.4), the **hugs and kisses** (fig.9.23) and the **stampato** (fig 9.24).

Fig. 9.23 Kisses & Hugs. *Photo: author.*   **Fig. 9.24** Stampato chain & photo: Stuller, Inc.

Fancy chain is typically hollow and designed for dress, rather than rough, every-day wear. Special care is required to prevent it from denting and scratching. (Repairing the dents may in fact be impossible.) Its price per gram is generally a bit higher than that of other chains. Since fancy chain is usually hollow and has a big look for its weight, the consumer may think it's less expensive.

Snake Chain

Snake chain is a sleek chain which looks like smooth, flexible metal from a distance (fig. 9.25). It may be rounded, square, rectangular or hexagonal. Snake chain is relatively strong, but will kink if it's bent repeatedly. Afterwards it's very difficult to repair. Sometimes it has a diamond-cut finish which makes it sparkle like diamond-cut rope chain. One manufacturer calls its diamond-cut white-gold snake chain "white-ice snake."

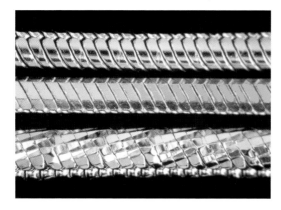

Fig. 9.25 Close-up view of gold snake chain. The one on the bottom is diamond-cut, white gold snake chain. *Photo by author.*

Bead Chain

Fig. 9.26 Bead chain and photo: Stuller, Inc..

As the name suggests, **bead chain** looks like metal beads strung on a wire. The beads may be round, oval, cylinder shaped or free-form. Bead chain can also be used to make spectacular necklaces like the one shown in figure 9.27. Bead chains offer a distinct shimmering look, but they're generally not as strong as link chains.

Other Neckwear Options

The range of options for wearing pendants is continually growing. Besides suspending them on chains, you can wear them on:

♦ **Neck wires** (also called **cable neck wires**). They may be single or multi-strand wires, and the wires may be parallel, coiled, or braided. The metal is typically stainless steel, silver, gold, or gold plated.

The thicker the wire and the more strands there are, the stronger the necklace. The weakest type of neck wire is **microwire**, which can be so thin that it's almost invisible, creating a unique effect when worn with a charm. Since its weight is so low, as low as 1 gram, its price can also be very low. The main disadvantages of microwire are that it kinks easily and it's not durable. Don't wear heavy pendants on microwire. Use a heavier wire or chain instead.

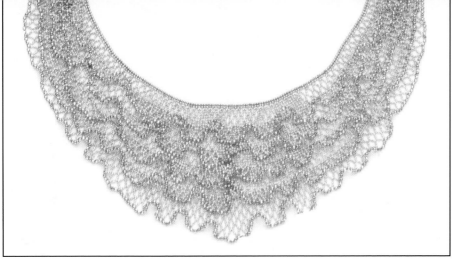

Fig. 9.27 Multi-layered ruffle necklace handcrafted by Christian Tse using tiny 18K gold beads with platinum trim. *Necklace and photo from Christian Tse.*

Fig. 9.28 Stainless steel multistrand wire necklaces with three diamond slides and detachable and interchangeable "Jeweldrops" by Barbara Westwood. The triangular stone is citrine, The black and gold piece is schist with iron pyrite. *Photo by Sky Hall.*

Fig. 9.29 Cord necklaces by Robert Wander for Winc Creations featuring green beryl, imperial topaz, watermelon tourmaline & aquamarine crystals. *Photo: J.Q. Magazine.*

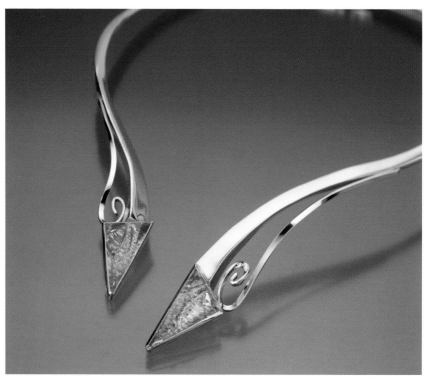

Fig. 9.30 Neckpiece with two unheated aquas carved by Sherris Cottier Shank. *Neckpiece by Christopher Jupp; photo by Robert Weldon.*

Fig. 9.31 Lapis beads over a clear rubber collar with a slider. *Jewelry and photo: The Bell Group.*

♦ **Cords or ribbons.** These may be of leather, rubber, vinyl, silk, satin, waxed cotton, rayon, satin, or other fabric and they may be braided or twisted. Cords and ribbons come in a multitude of colors which can be coordinated to your wardrobe and the gems worn with them.

♦ **Neck rings and neck collars**. They're rigid and fit around the neck like a collar. They may be tapered or non-tapered and the back may be open or have a clasp. Neck rings and collars with open backs are an option for people who have difficulty opening and closing clasps.

♦ **Woven collars**. These can have gemstone beads woven over a clear rubber cord.

Fig. 9.32 Cords and photo from Stuller, Inc.

Tips on Selecting Clasps

Ideally clasps are secure, attractive, easy to open and affordable for your budget. More often than not you can't choose clasps because they're already attached to chains, cords and necklaces. Nevertheless it's helpful to know something about clasps because sometimes you can select them, especially if you're having pearls or beads strung or if you're having a necklace or bracelet custom made. You can also have the clasp changed to a more appropriate style.

Some older people with arthritic hands have given up on wearing necklaces because they're unable to open and close them on their own. This is unfortunate and can be resolved by selecting larger clasps with a style that is easier to open. Here are the types of clasps from which you can choose:

♦ **Lobster clasp** or **lobster claw** (fig. 9.33). Secure, easy to open and relatively inexpensive, this is an ideal clasp for chains, cords and pearls. The larger the clasp, the easier it is to open. If the clasp is made of silver, stainless steel, or plated gold, the larger size won't have much of an impact on the price.

Fig. 9.33 Lobster clasp and photo from Stuller, Inc.

Fig. 9.34 Spring ring. *Photo by author.*

♦ **Spring ring** (fig. 9.34). This is a popular clasp for lightweight chains such as the box, cable or Singapore. It's typically the lowest priced clasp, but may not be very secure. Small spring rings may be difficult for some older people to open.

♦ **Push clasp** (fig. 9.35): The main advantage of this clasp is that it's fairly easy to open, even with one hand when it's used on a bracelet. It's also relatively inexpensive. Unfortunately, it's not as secure as some of the other clasps. However, a safety chain can be attached to make it more secure. Many push clasps are jewelry pieces by themselves and are best worn to the side or in the front of necklaces or on the top of bracelets.

Fig. 9.35 Push clasp and photo: Stuller.

There are several variations of the push clasp. One resembles a box and is therefore called the **box clasp** (fig. 9.36). Fancy chains often have a built-in box clasp. It can be tailored to the piece and may appear invisible from the top. Sometimes it's hard to find where to open the clasp, so be sure you try it out in the store.

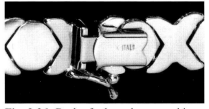

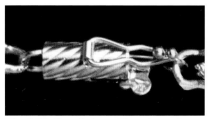

Fig. 9.36 Back of a box clasp on a kisses and hugs chain. *Photo by author.*

Fig. 9.37 Barrel clasp. *Photo by author.*

Another variation of the push clasp is the **barrel clasp** (fig. 9.37). Rope chains often come with barrel clasps. Sometimes people have a hard time determining how to open them and in the process damage the clasp. Be sure to try it a couple times in the store with the help of the salesperson. Occasionally these clasps come loose, so remember to close the safety lock.

♦ **Fish-hook clasp** (fig 9.38). Used mainly for pearls, this clasp is usually inexpensive and secure. The main drawback of the fish-hook clasp is that it can be hard to fasten and undo, especially for someone with arthritis or other dexterity problems.

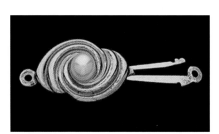

Fig. 9.38 Fish-hook clasp and photo from Stuller, Inc.

Fig. 9.39 Toggle clasp and photo from Stuller, Inc.

♦ **Toggle clasp** (fig. 9.39). This clasp consists of a bar that pushes through a loop to act as a fastener. It offers versatility and is often made of sterling silver or plated metal, but may also be made of gold.

♦ **Magnetic clasp** (figs. 9.41–9.44). This is a good option fo people with arthritic hands because it can be easily fastened and unfastened at the neck or wrist. However, it's not as secure as a lobster clasp or

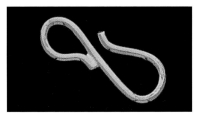

Figs 9.40–9.43 Open and closed views of magnetic clasps. *Photo & clasp from Stuller Inc.*

a clasp with a safety catch. Even though the magnets are strong, magnetic clasps are not recommended for heavy necklaces or necklaces with South Sea pearls or large, expensive gemstones. In most cases magnetic clasps can be worn with pacemakers, but it's best to consult your doctor first if you have a pacemaker.

Fig. 9.44 S-hook clasp and photo from Stuller, Inc.

♦ **Hook clasps** (fig. 9.45). As its name suggests, this clasp is a hook, which attaches to a small loop (hook and eye clasp) or a jump ring or some place on a strand of beads

Fig. 9.45 Hook clasp on a necklace from the Mahlia Jewelry Collection. *Photo by Robin Stancliff..*

or pearls. A variation of the regular hook clasp is the S-hook, which has the form of an "S." Hook clasps are most likely to be used with cords and hand-crafted neckwear. It's not uncommon for necklaces made in countries such as Indonesia to have hook clasps.

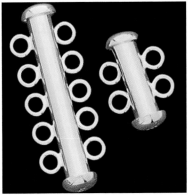

Figs. 9.46 & 9.47 Tube clasps (slide clasps) in closed position on the left and in partially open position on the right. *Clasps and photos from Stuller, Inc.*

♦ **Tube clasp** (figs. 9.46 & 9.47). Used primarily for multiple strands, this clasp is a two-part tube that's easy to use. You simply slide one end into the other to hold strands securely. This clasp is also called the **slide clasp**.

♦ **Foldover clasp** (fig. 9.48). Simple and secure, this clasp involves lifting up the top of a clasp, slipping it through a loop attached to a chain or strand, and then folding it over the loop.

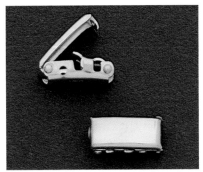

Fig. 9.48 Foldover clasp and photo from Stuller, Inc.

Fig. 9.49 Screw clasp (hidden bead clasp). *Clasp and photo from Stuller, Inc.*

♦ **Screw clasp** (fig. 9.49) This clasp can add versatility when it's inserted in pearls or beads to form a **mystery clasp.** For example, a long strand of pearls with three mystery clasps can be unscrewed and turned into a bracelet and two smaller necklaces. This clasp is also called a **hidden bead clasp.**

Screw clasps are fairly easy to open and close; they're also secure, if they're screwed in all the way and aren't stripped out. They tend to cost a little more than most of the other clasps.

Sometimes the string breaks on necklaces with mystery clasps. This can happen when people unscrew the clasp incorrectly or when they can't find the clasp and try to unscrew the necklace in a spot where there is no clasp. This problem can be avoided by having the jeweler show you how to find and open the clasp. When undoing it, be sure to grasp at least two pearls or beads on either side of the clasp. Turn them together as a unit. Don't simply twist the string.

When buying chains and necklaces, always check the clasp and know how it works. Ask the salesperson to show you how to open and close it. Then try it twice yourself. Make sure you're satisfied that it's not defective or too hard to operate.

Check that you hear a click when you close the safety lock. Then pull lightly on the chain to verify that the clasp is secure. If you plan to hang a pendant on the chain, make sure that it will fit over the clasp. If it doesn't, the clasp can often be changed. Inspect the clasp periodically, and when there's a problem, have it fixed before the clasp comes loose while you're wearing the chain.

If you're not satisfied with the clasp on a chain you like, it's usually easy to replace it with another style. Determine what is most important to you about the clasp because normally, some compromises will have to be made. For example, to get a clasp that is easy to open, you may have to accept less security and vice versa. For extra security, safety chains can be added.

10

Selecting Rings

In primitive times, the knot was a charm that was used to cast and bind a magic spell over people, and the first rings may have originated from knotted cords or wire placed around the finger.

In Egypt, the top part of the first ring was probably a signet, which was a seal used for officially marking documents. Later, the Egyptian custom of wearing rings was passed on to the Greek world. Greek rings were made of various materials including gold, silver, iron and ivory.

Besides serving as seals, ornaments and charms, rings have been used over the years as money, time-pieces, memorials for the dead, poison-filled weapons, receptacles for disinfectants and perfume, marks of authority and rank, badges of slavery, healing talismans, and passports to places of honor. Today, rings are often worn as a symbol of eternal commitment because their circular form has no beginning or end. In addition, they are like a knot around your finger which binds and reminds you of your commitment to a lover, spouse, friend, school, church, club or country.

The custom of placing a wedding ring on the fourth finger may have originated with the Egyptians. They believed a special vein or nerve ran from that finger to the heart. Another explanation for the custom is that it may have been a suggestion to women that they should be submissive to their future husbands since the fourth finger is the weakest one and can't be used independently. A third explanation is that placing the ring on the fourth finger may have been a way to avoid damaging the ring since it is the best-protected finger.

Aside from its symbol as an eternal commitment, a ring can be worn anytime anywhere without getting in the way, and you don't need a mirror to enjoy it. Today more money is spent on rings than on any other type of jewelry. Almost everybody wears a ring at some time in their life, so it's worthwhile to know what to look for when selecting one.

Selecting a Flattering Ring

Chapter 7 suggests that you select jewelry proportionate to your size. It also states that horizontal, vertical and diagonal line designs can help create illusions of lesser or greater length, width and size. These principles can also help you choose flattering rings.

If you want your rings to be in proportion to your fingers, don't select ones that extend beyond the width of your finger or past your lower or upper knuckles.

If you have a **small hand and short fingers**, a huge, broad ring can make your fingers look too short and your hand too small. To make your fingers look longer, choose a mounting with stones or lines arranged vertically or diagonally down the length of your finger. You could also wear simple rings with thinner bands.

If you have **long thin fingers**, you'll find that large broad rings, cluster styles, and round, square, and cushion-shape stones can all flatter your hands. A mounting with stones or lines flowing horizontally across your finger or that have height can make your hand appear shorter.

If you have **long broad hands**, a very small ring will tend to make them look bigger and won't have much impact. Therefore, a larger ring is preferable to a small ring.

If you have an **average-size hand**, almost any ring will look good on you. However, a ring that is too large can make your hand look smaller and defeat the advantage of having an ideal-size hand. Very thin delicate rings may go unnoticed and lack durability.

Practical Tips on Selecting Rings

When selecting a ring, you'll also want to consider comfort, durability and practicality. Let's discuss these factors one by one:

Comfort: No matter how good a ring looks, you probably won't wear it much if it's uncomfortable, so consider the following:

♦ **Can you bend your fingers easily when wearing the ring?** If not, the band may be too wide. Besides being uncomfortable, it could cause skin irritation due to collection of moisture and dirt under the band. If you like the wide broad-ring look, select a band that tapers down from a wide top to a narrow bottom so that your finger can bend freely.

♦ **Is the ring too tight or too loose?** This can be corrected by resizing the ring. If your band is more than 3/8" (10 mm) wide, it will probably need to be a half size larger than the size you normally wear in order to feel comfortable.

♦ **Does the ring feel rough and scratchy?** If the metal is irritating, it can usually be smoothed down by polishing. Occasionally, gemstones are set too low and the pointed bottoms prick your finger. If this is the case, it would probably be easier to choose another ring than to correct the problem.

♦ **Is the inner surface of the ring slightly rounded or completely flat?** A ring that is curved on the inside can conform to your finger better and therefore tends to be more comfortable. Men's wedding bands that are rounded inside are often sold under the trademarked name Comfort Fit™.

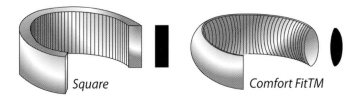

Fig. 10.1 Comfort fit ring diagrams from The Bell Group Rio Grande

Durability: The easiest way to test the strength of a ring is to squeeze it gently in your hand. If it bends or dents, it's not suitable for long-term, everyday wear. Always get permission from the jeweler or salesperson before doing this test. If they won't let you try the squeeze test, then it's an indication the piece is probably not very sturdy. Jewelers may use this test as an object lesson for customers; sometimes they will use it themselves to avoid buying flimsy merchandise.

Another test is to gently bounce the mounting in your hand and see how heavy it feels. If it's gold or platinum and it doesn't have a good solid feel, then it could be either hollow or too thin. Normally the more lightweight a piece is, the less durable it is unless it's made of a lightweight metal such as titanium, which is known for its low weight and superior strength.

Hollow jewelry presents a variety of problems. When the walls of the piece are thin, it dents and wears through quickly, leaving holes. Repairing it is difficult or impossible. Hollow rings are not easy to size. You can avoid a lot of possible distress by buying a solid every-day ring rather than a hollow one.

Very lightweight gold rings are cheaper because they have less gold in them. Buying mountings that are too thin, however, is shortsighted. The repairs on them later can end up costing more than the pieces themselves. Make sure the shank is solid and has an adequate thickness, at least 1.5 mm for an everyday ring. The prongs should not be too thin either, and ideally the setting will be secure and protect the stone well. See Chapter 5 for more information on settings.

A major advantage of platinum mountings is that they can normally be thinner and more delicate than those made of gold. This is because platinum is stronger and more dense than most gold alloys.

Practicality: Besides flattering your hand, a ring should be **suitable for your needs**. If it's for everyday or business wear, a simple style is often best. If it's for dressier occasions, you might want something fancier. No matter where you intend to wear your ring, there are some practical things to consider, so ask yourself the following questions:

♦ **If it has a setting, does it suit your lifestyle and level of activity?** Flush settings and full and partial-bezel settings are ideal for people who engage in contact sports or do manual labor. Pave, tension, or high-prong settings would not be a practical choice. See Chapter 5 for further information on settings.

♦ **If it has a center stone, does the ring stay in an attractive position as your hand moves or does it flop to the side?** This problem sometimes occurs when a large stone is mounted on a ring. It can be corrected by choosing a wider band or a band that is square or oval in shape on the outside instead of round. This problem can also occur if the ring is too big. Sizing balls inside the shank can help a ring stay in place on arthritic hands, which require oversize rings.

Figs. 10.2–10.13 An array of practical yet attractive ring styles from Stuller, Inc. The gemstones have been set level with the mountings using bezel setting, flush setting, channel setting, bar setting, or low prong setting. *Photos from Stuller, Inc.*

Fig. 10.14 Platinum and diamond rings by Eve J. Alfillé. Note the ring shapes and wave formation at the base of the shank, which help the rings stay in position on the finger. *Photo by Matthew Arden.*

Jewelry designer Eve Alfillé places a wave-like formation on the inside base of her rings. This is especially useful for people with large knuckles. The "waves" enable the wearer to tilt the ring and work it on. The wave fits the crease of the finger, and the ring stays on without spinning around the finger's thinner base. See figure 10.14.

Some of Alfillé's rings are squarish with rounded corners, both on the inside and outside of the ring. For people whose finger size varies a lot, the squared shank allows one full size leeway, whereas a round ring only allows a half size. A square shape like this follows the finger much more closely, but is much more difficult to achieve; there are no mandrels or sizers with that shape, so it is more costly in labor and requires at least one fitting before the stones are set.

♦ If you live in a cold climate and need to wear gloves, can you slip them on without damaging your ring or ripping the gloves?

♦ **Can the ring be sized easily?** Does your weight or finger size change frequently? If so, pay attention to the sizing factor and avoid, for example, eternity rings that have stones all around the band. Instead choose a ring where at least one third of the band is unset metal.

If you think your finger size could change by two or more sizes (this is unlikely), mention this to your jeweler and he will help you select an appropriate mounting. He'll probably suggest that you avoid rings with lots of baguette-shaped stones set up and down the sides of the mounting, and tension settings (settings that secure the stone with pressure on opposite sides rather than just metal). He'll also discourage you from buying titanium or tungsten rings, since they cannot be resized more than one-half size.

♦ **Does your jewelry tend to show lots of scratches?** People with active lifestyles often choose ring mountings with matte or brushed finishes because scratches and fingerprints are less noticeable. Matte (non-shiny) finishes can be added to any mounting. If you prefer the brilliance of a shiny finish, you can have the scratches polished away if they become obvious. A little of the metal, however, can wear away with repeated polishing.

♦ **Does the mounting style protect the center stone?** This is important for everyday rings. Ideally, if you accidentally hit your ring against walls or furniture, the contact will be with the metal of the ring and not the stones. If the stone(s) stick out past the contour of the ring, they're much more susceptible to damage than if they're recessed or set within the outline of the ring.

Determining Ring Size

One of the best ways to determine your ring size is to measure a ring that fits well on you. A ring can be measured more accurately than your finger because rings are hard metal objects unlike soft flesh and muscle. As a result, the method of wrapping a string or piece of paper around your finger and measuring it may not indicate a size that fits well. Nevertheless, the Table 1 size chart includes circumference measurements, which can help you estimate your ring size by measuring the length of a string or paper that encircles your finger.

If you're buying a ring through mail order or over the Internet, and don't know your size, you should first have a jeweler size your finger and/or measure ring(s) that fit well, even if you have to pay for the service. It's a waste of money to send rings back and forth through the mail because of improper fit. A major advantage of buying a ring in a jewelry store is that you can be assured before you buy it that it fits, looks good on you, and is comfortable.

Table 10.1 Ring Size Data (varies slightly from one source to another)

US ring size	Inside diameter in inches	Inside circum. in inches	Inside circum. in mm	Inside diameter in mm	JAP size	HK size	US size	UK size
2	.52	1.64	41.6	13.3	2	3	2	D
2.5	.537	1.69	42.8	13.7	3	5	2.5	E
3	.553	1.74	44.1	14.05	4	6	3	F
3.5	.57	1.79	45.4	14.45	5	7.5	3.5	G
							3.75	G.5
4	.585	1.84	46.7	14.86	7	9	4	H
							4.25	H.5
4.5	.602	1.89	48.0	15.27	8	10	4.5	I
							4.75	J
5	.618	1.94	49.2	15.70	9	11	5	J.5
							5.25	K
5.5	.634	1.99	50.5	16.10		12	5.5	K.5
					11			L.5
6	.650	2.04	51.8	16.52	12	13	6	M
6.5	.666	2.09	53.2	16.93	13	14.5	6.5	N
7	.683	2.14	54.3	17.32	14	16	7	O
7.5	.699	2.19	55.6	17.75	15	17	7.5	P
8	.715	2.24	56.9	18.18	16	18	8	Q
8.5	.731	2.29	60.7	18.56	17	19	8.5	Q.5
								R
9	.748	2.34	59.4	18.98	18	20.5	9	R.5
								S
9.5	.763	2.39	60.7	19.41	19	22	9.5	S.5
10	.78	2.44	62.1	19.84	20	23	10	T.5
10.5	.794	2.49	63.3	20.23	22	24	10.5	U.5
11	.81	2.54	64.5	20.60	23	25	11	V.5

Jewelers measure rings on a graduated ring stick. They usually use a set of steel rings in graduated sizes to measure the finger. Less expensive plastic sizing rings called finger gauges are also available (fig 10.15). The size systems can vary from one country or region to another. When determining your ring size, keep in mind the following:

♦ **Finger size can change throughout the day**. If possible, measure it at the end of the day when your fingers are usually largest. Measuring them on different days is also helpful.

♦ **Temperature affects finger size**. Heat expands, cold contracts. Therefore, don't measure finger sizes when your hands are cold. Let them warm up to room temperature.

♦ **The width of a ring is an important factor** in determining the best ring size. Wide rings often require a slightly larger size because they cover more of your finger. Because of this, many jewelers have two sizing ring sets—one narrow and one wide. However, the wide sizing rings may be hard to remove because often they're not polished well and don't slide off.

If you have difficulty removing a ring, try putting soap and water on the finger, or spray some window cleaner on the finger, unless the ring has a stone that can be damaged by ammonia. The window cleaner also helps clean the ring.

♦ **Your right and left hands normally have slightly different ring sizes**. The hand that you write with is typically about a half size larger that the non-primary hand.

♦ **Some metals cannot be sized because of their high strength.** Titanium and tungsten can't be downsized, and titanium can only be stretched about a half size. Consequently it's very important that the ring size be accurate when buying rings made of these metals. An example of a ring stretcher is shown in figure 10.16.

If the rings are too big, metal strips called ring guards (fig. 10.18) can be placed inside the ring to make it smaller.

Another way of reducing the size of a ring is to apply a special adhesive (fig. 10.17). It dries to a solid clear soft plastic, providing a secure fitting ring with no visible plastic or metal showing on the outer surface of the band. The plastic ring guard can be removed by peeling it off.

Fig. 10.15 Plastic finger gauge for determining ring size. *Finger sizers and photo from Grobet USA.*

Fig. 10.17 An adhesive for reducing the size of a ring. *Ring Guard and photo from FDJ On Time LLC.*

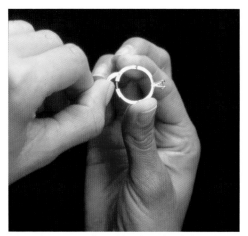

Fig. 10.19 An adjustable ring shank by Finger Fit®—ideal for people with big knuckles. *Photo & shank from The Bell Group Rio Grande.*

Fig. 10.16 A combination ring stretcher, reducer and bender. *Ring stretcher and photo from Jemco Jewelers Supply.*

Fig. 10.18 Ring guard. It fits inside the shank of the ring to make the ring tighter. *Ring guard and photo from Stuller Inc.*

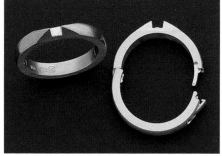

Fig. 10.20 Superfit® hinged shank. A push button opening allows your ring to clasp snugly around your finger. *Ring shank and photo from Stuller Inc.*

If you're buying the ring as a surprise gift, you have a few options for determining the size. If the ring is of gold or platinum and you get it from a nearby jewelry store that can easily size it, buy the ring in its existing size and then have it sized to fit. There's no point in having it sized twice.

You can also ask the recipient's mother or friend if they know the size or have a ring that fits the recipient's finger. Afterwards, a jeweler can measure the ring. If you're in a jewelry store with the recipient, suggest that he or she have their ring(s) cleaned. Stores will usually do this for free. Then secretly ask the salesperson to check the ring size.

The average woman's American ring size ranges about 5½ to 7. The average men's size ranges from about 9 to 11. Table 10.1 lists the inside diameter and circumference values that correspond to ring sizes in various countries. Keep in mind that the numerical values are not absolute and vary a little from one source to another. Even ring measuring gauges are not all calibrated exactly the same way.

Some people have given up wearing rings because they have large or arthritic knuckles. If they do slip on a ring, it's usually too big and twists around on their fingers. There are solutions to this. One type of device that corrects this problem is the adjustable ring shank by Finger Fit®, which can be soldered to the bottom half of the ring (see figure 10.19). If the shank has been made to a size 6, for example, it can open to a size 9.

Another option for people with large knuckles is the Superfit® shank (fig 9.20). It opens to a large size on a hinge and closes safely to a smaller size becoming virtually invisible. For more information on adjustable rings, consult your local jeweler.

Fig 11. 1 Pierced stud earrings.
Earrings & photo: Stuller, Inc.

Fig. 11.2 Screw-in post studs.
Earrings & photo: Stuller, Inc.

Fig. 11.3 Screw-back close-up view. *Photo by author.*

Fig. 11.4 Screw-back earrings for people who don't have pierced ears. *Photo by the author.*

Fig.11.5 Clip-on earrings. *Photo by the author.*

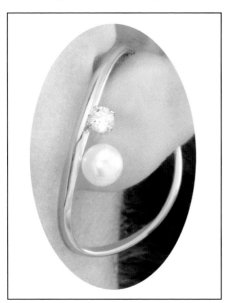

Fig. 11.6 Earrings that hook on the ears from HOOKer Earrings. *Photo by Jeff LeFever.*

Fig. 11.7 HOOKer Earrings by Barbara Barnett *Photo by Jeff LeFever.*

11

Selecting Earrings

The oldest earrings ever unearthed by archaeologists date to about 2,500 B.C. and were discovered in Ur, Iraq in the stone coffin of a monarch. Prior to 1600 A.D., it was just as fashionable for men to wear earrings as for women. Julius Caesar was especially fond of them. In the 13th century in Persia, earrings were so popular that kings had engravings of themselves, wearing their earrings, set as signet stones in their rings.

Over the centuries, earrings have gone in and out of style depending on the type of hairdos and clothing worn at the time. If the ears were covered, there was no point in wearing earrings. When the ears are exposed, earrings can affect one's facial appearance more than any other type of jewelry.

The effect earrings have or the ways they can flatter you will be discussed later in the chapter. But first let's discuss the different types of earrings.

Earring Types and Styles

There are four basic ways of attaching ear ornaments to one's ear:

♦ Piercing the ear and inserting a wire or post through the hole (**pierced earrings**) (figs. 11.1 & 2)

♦ Screwing a small circular clamp next to the back of the ear without a wire or post going through the ear (**screw-backs**) (figs. 11.3 & 4)

♦ Clipping the earrings onto the ear (**clip-ons**) (fig 11.5)

♦ Hooking the earring into the ear or around the ear (**hook-ons**) (figs. 11.6 & 7)

The pierced earring may have been the first type of ear ornament. One notable person who wore them was King Tutankhamun. Pierced earrings are currently the most popular type.

Little is known about the origins of hooking ear ornaments in or around one's ear, and many people are unaware that such earrings exist. However, for people like myself who don't want pierced ears, hook-on earrings are an ideal alternative. When they fit properly, they're comfortable and they're very secure in the ear. The types I wear are patented and are called HOOKer™ earrings.

The screw-back earring was invented in the early 1900's and was very popular until the 1930's, when the clip-on appeared on the market. Since it fit more securely to the ear than the screw-back, the clip-on became the number one choice of earring.

By the 1970's, pierced earrings had made a comeback, and they still are the primary type of earring on the market. The ear attachment may be a smooth, threaded, or friction ear post with an ear nut at the end, or they may be a smooth or threaded wire, which may have a lever back or a clip called an omega clip or French clip (figs. 11.8–11.13).

When threaded posts screw into an ear nut, they are sometimes called "screw-backs," but this is not the original meaning of the term. Some jewelers recommend threaded posts for security, but others do not like them. For example, Eve Alfillé, a jeweler in Evanston, Illinois, has found that some of the earlier threaded posts are heavier, or thicker (18Gauge) than our ears in the U.S. are pierced for, and therefore can be uncomfortable. The newer ones are the regular 20 Gauge thickness, but that sacrifices strength; the thread of the screw will become stripped sooner or later. Every time you wrestle the screws in, you could be in fact repiercing your ear—not a comfortable experience. As a result, Alfille now always redirects her customers to the much gentler and safer "Poussette" backs. They have a smooth post with two grooves, onto which fits a well-made, substantial domed back which is activated by depressing two levers.

A similar post is called the Guardian. Eve recommends the ones with the two levers, not just one. They are more expensive, but well worth it. They exist in 14 and 18 karat gold, and in platinum.

Figs. 11.8–11.13 Types of pierced earrings: ear wires, post earrings, omega clips, hinged earrings and lever-back ear wires. *Earrings from King.Plutarco, Inc.; photos by Diamond Graphics.*

There are many styles of pierced earrings, which include:

♦ **Hoop earrings**. These have a circular shape that go under the lobes, and they come in varying widths (figs.11.15–17). Hoops were among the first types of earrings.

♦ **Dangle, pendant, drop, or chandelier earrings**. Sometimes the terms are used interchangeably, and other times they are used to refer to distinct types of earrings that hang below the ear. Dangles and chandeliers usually have loose designs that move and have more than one component. Sometimes they attach to a button or cluster.

♦ **Bar earring**: A metal bar that hangs down from the ear and is often set with gemstones

♦ **Stud**: A small, simple ear-ring usually made of a solid metal or gem. Metal, pearl or diamond studs can be worn with anything. For variety, a stud can be worn with an **earring jacket**, which is a detachable jew-elry piece worn around or attached to a stud to pro-

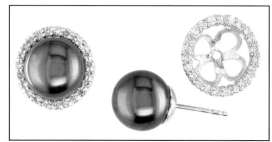

Fig. 11.14 Stud earring & jacket from A & Z Pearls. *Photo by Diamond Graphics.*

vide a different look. The jacket has a hole or tiny loop for the stud post and may be found in simple to elaborate styles consisting only of metal or set with gems.

♦ **Button earring**: A single flat or domed piece that's often round, but may be of other shapes such as oval, square or heart shaped

♦ **Cluster earring**: An earring with a group of gems forming the design

♦ **Fashion earring**: A general term for earrings with various designs and motifs such as flowers, shells, animals, feathers, knots, abstract designs, etc. Often they're simply identified as earrings.

Selecting Flattering Earrings

When you wear earrings, they become a part of the contour of your face. Therefore, it's helpful to consider your facial shape when selecting earrings. Those that counteract your face shape tend to be the most

Figs. 11.15–11.28 Earring styles including hoop, dangle, bar, drop, stud, cluster, button and fashion. *Earrings and photos from Stuller, Inc.*

flattering. For example, earnings with curved lines can soften the appearance of an angular face. The face shapes that were discussed in Chapter 7 are listed below along with earring recommendations.

Oval: Almost any style earring goes well with this facial shape. If it's long, button earrings or hoops can help increase the appearance of width.

Round: Oblongs, rectangles, semi-circles and straight dangles are good options for round faces. Angular designs and elongated shapes can help to slim a full face. If you want to de-emphasize the roundness, avoid large round earrings or those that merely follow the lines of the ear lobe. Choose instead, designs with vertical lines, which will make the face appear more oval.

Square: Oval, oblong or semi-circular earrings are best. Square and cushion-shapes that sit on the ear make it look wider. Drop and dangle earrings can elongate both the face and neck, provided the dangles are not too long. Generally the most flattering earrings for square faces are those that are curved and longer than they are wide.

Rectangular: Round styles, hoops or any curved designs that add width are ideal. Elongated drops, bars and dangles tend to emphasize face length.

Heart shape: Triangles and other shapes that are wider at the bottom than at the top are especially flattering to the heart-shape face. Round hoops with their curves can soften the point of the chin. Long narrow earrings add length and accentuate the pointedness of the chin.

The size and shape of your ear lobes can affect the appearance and choice of your earrings. Button-type or geometric-shaped clips can minimize very large or small ear lobes.

If you wear eyeglasses, and you like to wear earrings, it's good to select plain basic frames that will not compete with your jewelry. Simple-style earrings may also be preferable. Wear your glasses when you try on the earrings and see how they look together.

When choosing earrings, get the complete effect by looking at them in the mirror from the front, back and sides. Consider them in relation to your hairdo and the clothing and eyeglasses with which they will be worn. When properly chosen, earrings can do more to bring out your best facial features than any other jewelry.

12

Selecting Bracelets

The word "bracelet" comes from the French word *bras,* which means "arm." Today bracelets are primarily worn at the wrist for decoration, but in early times, warriors wore them high on the forearm and above the biceps for functional purposes. They believed that tight bands around their arms gave them added strength for manipulating their shields and swords during battle.

Women were more likely to wear bracelets closer to the wrist. However, in some parts of Asia, bracelets encircled their entire arm and were worn as indications of wealth and rank.

The earliest bracelets among the ancient Egyptians were solid bands of plain or enameled metal. Bracelets set with colored gemstones and diamonds were popularized by the Mogul Emperors of India. In China, bracelets cut out of a single piece of jade became prized. The Chinese have long believed that jade brings prosperity and embodies the Confucian virtues of wisdom, justice, compassion and courage. In some regions of China, jade bracelets are thought to protect against rheumatism.

One of the most popular bracelets of modern times is the tennis bracelet. It got its name when Chris Evert, a famous tennis player, attracted public attention to it. Her straight-line bracelet came off during a televised match. Evert stopped the match to pick it up, and afterwards, called it her tennis bracelet. The name became part of jewelry history. The rest of this chapter discusses other types of bracelets and gives tips on selecting them.

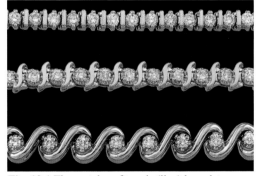

Fig. 12.1 Three styles of tennis (line) bracelets. *Bracelets and photo from Stuller, Inc.*

Bracelet Types

There are four basic types of bracelets:

♦ **Bangle**: A stiff circular or oval band that slips over the hand (fig. 12.4). Sometimes the outside of the bracelet is angular in shape like a square. The bangle may be of one piece or it may have a hinged clasp, which either opens or loosens the bracelet for putting on and removal. Often the clasp is hidden, making the bangle appear like a solid piece. Fine-quality hinged bangles usually feature short safety chains in case their clasp opens accidentally. Bangles vary in width and can be worn in pairs or groups.

♦ **Cuff**: A stiff bracelet that has an opening in the back that slips over the wrist (figs. 12.2 and 12.8). It usually fits tighter to the wrist than a bangle. When putting on a cuff bracelet, slip it on sideways over the smallest part of your wrist so it will remain the proper size.

♦ **Flexible bracelet**: A bendable bracelet consisting of interlocked links or a series of motifs (figs. 12.3 and 12.9). The straight-line tennis bracelet is an example. It's also called a **line bracelet** (figs. 12.1). Medical ID bracelets are often flexible. They're engraved with the wearer's personal medical problems or history and can speak for the wearer when he or she can't. (Pendants on necklaces can also be used for this purpose.)

♦ **Chain bracelet**: If the bracelet has chain which alternates with gems, beads or pearls, it's called a **station bracelet** (fig 12.5). If the chain has attached charms, it's called a **charm bracelet** (fig. 12.6).

Most bracelets are worn at the wrist, but arm and ankle bracelets are also available.

Tips on Selecting Bracelets

Opinions differ as to which is the most flattering type of bracelet. Some fashion experts recommend that you choose a bracelet that's in proportion to your arm and wrist. For example, they believe that small-boned people should select delicate bracelets, whereas people with large wrists should wear large, wide bracelets.

Fig 12.2 Cuff bracelet of 18K yellow gold set with diamond macles, raw diamond cubes and rough rubies. *Forged and fabricated by Todd Reed: photo by Hap Sakwa.*

Fig. 12.3 Hinged flexible bracelet hand fabricated by Todd Reed with 18K yellow, green, white and rose gold and 8mm raw diamond cubes. *Photo by azadphoto.com.*

Fig. 12.4 Hinged sterling silver bangle bracelet by Todd Reed set with raw diamond cubes. *Photo by azadphoto.com.*

Fig. 12.5 18K yellow gold bracelet with hand fabricated chain and raw diamond cubes. *Bracelet by Todd Reed; photo by azadphoto.com.*

Fig. 12.6 Charm bracelet wtih carved jade, smoky quartz, and porcelain beads. *Bracelet and photo from Sajen™.*

Fig. 12.7 Bracelet sizers. *Gauges and photo from FDJ On Time LLC.*

Fig. 12.8 Sterling silver cuff bracelet with barrel race rodeo scene. *Bracelet and photo from The Bell Group Rio Grande.*

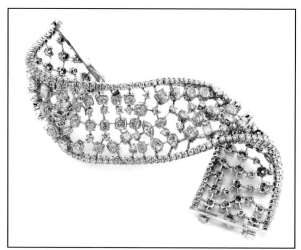

Fig.12.9 Flexible bracelet set with yellow and pink diamonds. *Bracelet from King Plutarco, Inc; photo by Diamond Graphics.*

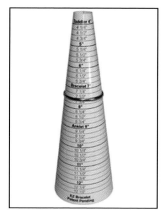

Fig. 12.10 Bracelet sizer and photo from FDJ On Time, LLC.

Jeweler James Avery would disagree. In his book *The Right Jewelry for You*, he says that a narrow bangle works well for people with broad wrists. If they want to wear larger, bolder bracelets, Avery recommends that they wear bracelets with an open-work or latticed design because they appear to have less volume and do not broaden one's wrist. Avery thinks that if you have slender wrists, you can wear any type of bracelet as long as it doesn't overpower you or look so insignificant that it has no impact. However, if your wrist is thin, look for bracelets that are smaller in diameter because they will make the wrist seem broader in proportion.

One advantage of buying a bracelet in a jewelry store is that you can try it on to see how it fits and looks. If you're buying by mail order or on the Internet, measure your dominant wrist (usually the right wrist) where your watch is worn. If you don't have a tape measure, wrap a string or piece of paper around your wrist and measure it. The paper or string should be loose enough so you can put a finger between it and your wrist. Check the length with a ruler and ask the seller what bracelet size the measurement corresponds to.

A more accurate way of determining bracelet size is with a bracelet sizer (fig. 12.10) or sizing bracelets, which are similar to sizing rings (fig. 12.7).

When selecting a bracelet, it's also important to consider how sturdy it is because bracelets get knocked on furniture, counters and walls. Mountings that look big and heavy but feel light are apt to be hollow. It's a good idea to always ask if a piece is hollow. Salespeople should tell you this without being asked, but they don't always do so. Hollow jewelry presents a variety of problems. When the walls of the piece are thin, it dents and wears through quickly, leaving holes. Repairing it is difficult or impossible.

Hollow bangle bracelets can be sturdy while still being more comfortable than a solid one of the same size. The key is the thickness of the metal. You shouldn't be able to dent it with pressure from your fingertips. If it's made of gold, it should feel substantial in weight. If you're in the market for a hollow bangle bracelet, you may wish to consider buying one of the twisted metal styles. The multiple ridges make the bracelet stronger and more rigid, and they help hide signs of wear.

13

Brooches, Pins & Clips

According to Random House Webster's College Dictionary (2000), a **brooch** is "a clasp or ornament having a pin at the back for passing through clothing and a catch for securing the point of the pin" whereas a **pin** ornament would typically just have a slender piece of wire with a pin at the end attached to the ornament. Many jewelers, however, also call brooches pins, and they may use the term "**stick pin**" to distinguish straight long pins with ornamental tips from brooches. ("Brooch" can also be spelled the way it sounds—broach.)

Some members of the trade, however, do not use the terms "brooch" and "pin" interchangeably. For example, Elise Misiorowski, a jewelry historian and the director of the GIA museum, says "I have always thought that the difference between a brooch and a pin with a clasp is determined by the size of the piece, and the importance of materials. In the 19th century, small pins with clasps were made for use on ladies undergarments. I would categorize those as pins. They came in matching sets of gold, often enameled and set with small seed pearls, in different sizes from ¾ – 1½". Additionally, small 'lace' pins were used to fasten tulle or lace to the front of the dress bodice or to enhance a veil on a hat. To me, brooches are generally larger than two inches and are typically set with more gems [that are] juicy and opulent (fig.13.1). There are times, however, when a pin could be called a brooch, and that would be if it is set with important gems."

Pins were in use as far back as 1000 B.C. Their primary purpose was to fasten clothing. Even today they may have the same purpose. Many of these pins looked like the modern-day safety pin and were called *fibulae*. A pin is still used to hold together Scottish kilts, but more often than not, pins are worn for decoration. They've also been worn as good luck charms and as badges of courage or love. For instance, "sweetheart brooches," which were sent to loved ones, were very popular with the British Army.

Pins and brooches are sometimes worn to show support or express thoughts and feelings. Flag pins became popular after the September 11 World Trade Center attacks as a symbol of patriotism and sympathy. Madeleine Albright, former US Secretary of State, often wore brooches and pins that were appropriate to the message of the day. For example, when speaking to the military, she wore a pin combining the insignia of America's five armed services. The pin might be a balloon when she was feeling up, a spider if she was feeling devious, a bee if she was looking for someone to sting, or the Capitol building to show bipartisanship. Albright told reporters looking for news to "read her pins" (pg. 343 of *Madam Secretary* by Madeleine Albright).

In the 1920's, Cartier replaced the hinged pin with a **clip**—a metal plate operated by a spring that allowed the plate to clasp the fabric. Later two parallel metal pins were used to make the clip lighter and more versatile. The clip could be placed so as to accentuate any desired part of a dress—the neckline, lapel, side or waistline. Sweater clips and shoe clips may be functional as well as decorative.

In the 1930's the double clip became popular. This was a combination of two identical clips, which could be attached to a fitting making made them wearable as a single brooch (figs. 13.3 to 13.6).

Brooches, pins and clips draw attention to the area where they are placed. Therefore, if you want to de-emphasize an area such as the bust line, do not place a brooch there. If you have a large or tall figure and you want your brooch to make an impact, select one that's in proportion to your size rather than a small delicate piece.

A brooch is a great way to dress up a basic outfit. In fact, brooches usually look their best on single color fabrics. Brooches, pins and clips are probably the most versatile types of jewelry. Photos in this chapter and the next one show a few ways in which they can be worn.

Fig. 13.1 Eagle brooch set with diamonds, blue sapphires, rubies and emeralds. *Brooch from Joseph DuMouchelle Auctioneers; photo by David Behl.*

Fig. 13.2 Retro 14K yellow gold and cultured pearl pin from Joseph DuMouchelle Auctioneers. *Photo by Dave Frechette.*

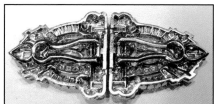

Figs. 13.3 and 13.4 The front and back of a double-clip diamond brooch, which is shown below separated into individual clips, also called sweater clips. They can be worn separately at the corners of a sweater or joined to close a sweater like a button would. *Brooch from Karen McGinn; photos by Karen McGinn.*

Fig. 13.5 Diamond clips detached from brooch above. *Photo by Karen McGinn.*

Fig. 13.6 Same diamond clips worn on a dress. *Photo by Karen McGinn.*

Style Tips from an Antique Jewelry Expert

♦ For a classic look, wear a white-metal diamond/pearl brooch—ideally Edwardian era (1890–1915)—on a white/off-white suit or shirt. Earrings should be either diamond or pearl.

Fig. 13.7 Edwardian diamond, platinum and white gold brooch from Joseph DuMouchelle Auctioneers. *Photo by Hong Choi.*

♦ Brooches and large non-dangle earrings work well together, but an Edwardian pin and chandelier earrings do not; use either one or the other.

♦ Brooches look out of place and distracting with a 16-inch necklace, but acceptable with a longer single strand necklace or chain. If you wear a double or triple strand necklace, don't wear a brooch.

♦ Solid metal brooches look good on outer coats.

♦ Let the fabric dictate the weight of the pin. Multiple pins form a cluster on a cashmere jacket; consider wearing a single pin of tiny pearls on a linen jacket.

♦ A multicoloured pin can enhance a multicoloured scarf, provided one colour matches.

♦ Wear a diamond brooch at the center of the "V" neck on a formal.

♦ Double clips look good at the ends of spaghetti straps.

♦ It's okay to mix jewelry periods, but keep the end result in mind.

The above tips are from Debra Sawatsky, GG, ISA-CAPP, an appraiser and specialist in antique and period estate jewelry in Toronto, Canada.

Debra's grandmother has one final tip:

♦ Get dressed with everything you like—then remove one item.

Fig 13.8 Nineteenth century antique diamond, yellow gold, silver and enamel butterfly pin from Joseph DuMouchelle Auctioneers. *Photo by Melinda Adducci.*

Fig. 13.9 Tsavorite garnet and yellow sapphire bee pin from Timeless Gem Designs. *Photo by Rachelle Sarosi.*

Figs. 13.10 and 13.11 Front and back of a pair of shoe clips. Even though certain wealthy people may wear diamond shoe clips, most are costume jewelry like these. They are shown below on shoes. *Clips from Karen McGinn; photos by Karen McGinn.*

Fig. 13.13 Scottish rite kilt pin from Joseph DuMouchelle Auctioneers. *Photo by David Frechette.*

Fig. 13.12 Same clips on shoes. *Photo by Karen McGinn.*

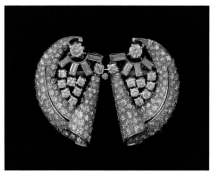

Fig. 13.14 Art Deco platinum and diamond double clip brooch from Joseph DuMouchelle Auctioneers. *Photo by David Behl.*

Fig. 13.15 Art Deco platinum, diamond, ruby and emerald lapel watch and pin from Joseph DuMouchelle Auctioneers. *Photo by Melinda Adducci.*

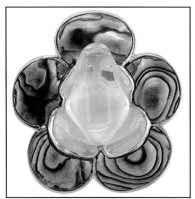

Fig. 13.16 Crystal frog paua shell pin/pendant. *Pin and photo from Sajen™.*

Fig. 13.18 Platinum and diamond pearl shortener/pin from Joseph Du-Mouchelle Auctioneers. The shortener slides off to be worn alone as a pin. *Photo by Hong Choi.*

Fig. 13.17 White gold diamond pin/enhancer from Timeless Gem Designs. *Photo by Rachelle Sarosi.*

14

Making Jewelry Versatile

One piece of jewelry can serve many functions. For example, a brooch or a clip can be used to:

♦ Fasten a dress, robe, or blouse

♦ Hold up a sleeve or cuff

♦ Gather a scarf into folds

♦ Act as a pearl shortener (a hinged ring used to shorten a long strand)

Even when simply used as ornaments, brooches, pins and clips can be worn or displayed in a variety of places such as:

♦ Near the neckline; at the side, center or collar of a dress, jacket, sweater, shirt or blouse

♦ On a pocket

♦ On a hat

♦ At the waistline or on a belt

♦ On a tie, scarf or shawl

♦ On a necklace or strand of beads or pearls at the front, side or back. Some pins and clips are specifically designed for this purpose and may be called pin/enhancers or pin/pendants.

♦ On a bracelet

♦ On a ring

♦ On a band or ribbon in the hair

♦ At the top or bottom of the ear if they're ear clips

♦ On a purse

♦ On the shoes

♦ On a present

♦ On a lampshade

One piece of jewelry can also have many looks. Earrings with jackets and/or detachable dangles or pendants are one of the best examples. The hanging part can be removed for business or less formal occasions.

Figs. 14.1 to 14.3 Cultured pearl and diamond earrings that can be worn with or without dangles or jackets. *Earrings from A & Z Pearls; photos by Diamond Graphics.*

EASY AS.....

1.

2.

3.

Figs. 14.4 and 14.5 Carved flower earring jackets by Timeless Gem Designs. This collection of flowers made of jasper, agate, mother of pearl, black onyx, sodalite and other gemstones can work together to create the right blossom to go with any outfit. These jackets can also be worn with diamond or pearl studs. *Photos by Rachelle Sarosi.*

Figs. 14.6 & 14.7 Hooker earrings with removable dangles available with various gems. *Photos by Jeff LeFever.*

Fig. 14.8 Removable South Sea pearl drops on diamond earrings by King Plutarco. *Photo by Diamond Graphics.*

Another way to make jewelry versatile is to make it reversible. This can be done with bracelets, necklaces, earrings and pendants.

Fig. 14.9 Labradorite and detailed silver swirls reversible pendant. *Pendant and photo from Sajen™.*

Fig. 14.10 Labradorite and paua shell reversible pendant. *Jewelry and photo from Sajen™.*

Convertible jewelry is not new. Versatility was common with older pieces—look for hidden or removable bales or pin attachments. Some examples from estate collections are below.

Fig 14.11 Removable center clips on an 18K gold, diamond and emerald Gubelin bracelet. The two clips can be worn as pins. *Bracelet from Joseph DuMouchelle Auctioneers; photo David Behl.*

Fig. 14.12 Diamond & pearl ring/ pin from Joseph DuMouchelle Auctioneers. Pin top slides into ring frame to convert to ring. *Photo by Hong Choi.*

Fig. 14.13 Diamond circle bow pin/pendant from Joseph DuMouchelle Auctioneers. *Photo by Hong Choi.*

Fig 14.14 A hinged pear shape cover converts this Hamilton platinum and diamond watch into an attractive bracelet. *Watch from Joseph DuMouchelle Auctioneers; photo by David Behl.*

Strands of beads or pearls can have special clasps such as the mystery clasp, hook clasp or oyster clasp, which allow them to be worn in different ways. Figure 14.15 shows a hook clasp on one end of a Tahitian pearl strand, which can be attached at various places on the pearl strand creating distinct styles. The versatility of the oyster clasp is shown on the opposite page.

Fig 14.15 The hook clasp on this dyed freshwater pearl necklace can be attached anywhere on the strand, creating versatility. *Necklace by Konstantina Mahlia; photo by Robin Stancliff.*

Figs. 14.16 & 14.17 Indian Fishnet Choker/Handlet. This necklace (made for Goldie Hawn) detaches at the sides to become a bracelet and a "handlet", which attaches to a matching ring. *Jewelry © 2006 by Carolyn Tyler; photos by R & R Photography.*

Figs 14.18–14-22 Five of the necklace styles made possible by a 32–36" strand of pearls or beads and the oyster clasp from A & Z Pearls. The size of the pearls or beads dictates the design of the clasp. *The photos on the left are by Diamond Graphics. The above photo is from A & Z Pearls.*

Fig. 14.23 Oyster clasp—a hinged clasp designed for versatility. *Clasp and pearls from A & Z Pearls; photo by Richard Rubins.*

Fig. 14.25 Close-up view of another side of the tree at left made by Ellen Streit. *Photos by author.*

New uses for costume jewelry

A chiropractor friend received this jewelry tree, which was made from costume jewelry worn by two of her patients, a mother and daughter-in-law. The daughter-in-law, Ellen Streit, designed and made the tree and it was given as a Christmas present. My friend treasures this jewelry tree and keeps it on display in her living room. Costume jewelry has also been used to decorate picture and mirror frames.

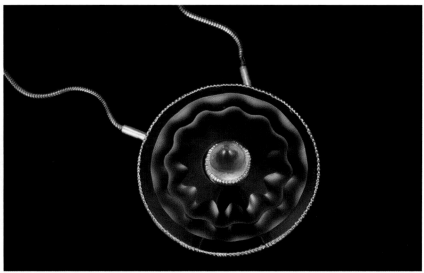

Fig. 14.26 Citrine and black jade cut and carved by Lew Wackler and designed as a teapot lid and pendant by Todd Reed. *Photo by azadphoto.com.*

Fig. 14.27 Sterling silver and 18K yellow gold teapot with lid in fig. 14.26. *Teapot & lid by Todd Reed; photo by azadphoto.com.*

As you can see, the possible uses of jewelry pieces are endless. If you have jewelry you never wear, use your imagination. You might be able to find unique ways of wearing them or using them that are not even mentioned in this chapter.

Fig. 15.1 Titanium and 18K yellow gold inlay ring with a matte finish on the outside. *Ring & photo from The Bell Group.*

Fig. 15.2 Flush-set diamond ring in 18K white & yellow gold. *Ring & photo from Mark Schneider.*

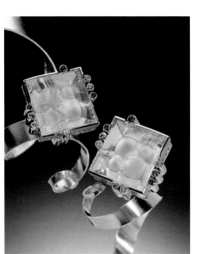

Fig. 15.3 Fantasy-cut rutilated quartz 18K gold cufflinks by Mark Schneider. *Photo by John Parrish.*

Fig. 15.4 One-of-a-kind crescent moon faces hand carved in black agate in Idaroberstein, Germany and set in 18K gold. The cufflinks from Timeless Gem Designs can be personalized with the profiles of family members or pets. *Photo by Rachelle Sarosi.*

Fig. 15.5 A sturdy solid-link chain, medical ID bracelet. *Gents 14K yellow gold bracelet and photo from Stuller, Inc.*

15

Jewelry Tips for Men

Men tend to be harder on jewelry than women. Consequently, it's important that their jewelry be able to withstand more wear. Here are some tips on selecting sturdy jewelry that will last:

♦ **Select rings and bracelets with a substantial amount of metal.** Mountings that are too thin can break and bend; over time, the metal can even wear away. Rings and bracelets are especially susceptible to damage because they get knocked and scraped. Pins, earrings and tie tacs can be more fragile. Make sure that rings are not so thick that they dig into your skin and hurt when you grasp items such as shovels and brooms. Some jewelers advise men to get comfort-fit rings, which have rounded edges on the shank to prevent discomfort.

♦ **Avoid hollow jewelry,** especially rings and bracelets. They can dent and form holes when the metal wears away. Even though hollow jewelry can be repaired, it may not look like new afterwards. If there's a hole or break at one point, there's likely to be a weakness elsewhere. Repairs can become a never-ending process. Instead, buy solid rings, bracelets and chains.

To determine if a piece is hollow, ask the sales person. You can also gently bounce the mounting in your hand to see how heavy it feels. If it's gold or platinum and doesn't have a good, solid feel, then it's probably either hollow or too thin. Normally the more lightweight a piece is, the less durable it is. Lightweight pieces are cheaper because they have less gold, platinum or palladium. Buying mountings that are too thin, however, is shortsighted. The repairs on them later can end up costing more than the pieces themselves.

♦ **Select low settings.** Bezel and flush-settings usually offer the most protection for gems (fig. 15.2). High-prong settings and pavé settings with small stones are not good choices for men's everyday rings. (See Chapter 5, "Selecting the Setting.")

Fig. 15.6 *Coeur de Lion* coat of arms signet rings by Gem Shapes, Inc. They're individually hand engraved in intaglio form with your family coat of arms. *Rings and photo from Joseph DuMouchelle Auctioneers.*

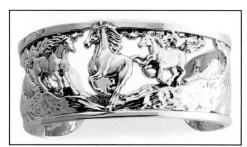

Fig. 15.7 Sterling silver cuff. *Bracelet and photo from The Bell Group Rio Grande.*

Fig. 15.8 Bola tie by Mark Schneider. It features a tanzanite, black pearl, white pearl, yellow and white diamonds, citrine and black jade. *Photo by John Parrish.*

Fig. 15.9 Mother of pearl gambling counter, hand engraved with a Chinese scene and set in a sterling silver money clip by Timeless Gem Design. *Photo by Rachelle Sarosi.*

♦ **Consider buying rings with non-shiny, textured finishes**. They are less likely to show scratches, nicks and other signs of wear than surfaces with a high polish.

♦ **Select durable gemstones for rings and bracelets**. For example, diamond, jade, ruby, sapphire, cat's-eye, alexandrite and spinel are better choices for men's rings than emerald, tanzanite, malachite, moonstone and coral.

What Types of Jewelry Do Men Wear?

While researching this book, I asked several jewelers what types of jewelry men wear most. Rings and watches seem to be the most popular. However, cufflinks are making a comeback; and depending on one's cultural heritage, neck-chains, bracelets and pendants may also be commonly worn. Other jewelry items are belt buckles, pins, tie tacs, bola ties and earrings.

Titanium and tungsten jewelry is a growing market with men because of its high durability and resistance to wear. However, as jeweler Paul Cassarino warns, "customers should be aware that rings made of titanium, tungsten carbide or stainless steel cannot be sized or adjusted should the owner's finger size change. Some companies will allow an exchange with partial credit given for the used ring. However, that would not be suitable for wedding rings since most owners would not ever consider trading in the ring that was blessed at their wedding ceremony."

Some jewelers said that men often prefer personalized jewelry that's related to their family, hobbies, profession, clubs, and places where they live. For example, their jewelry may feature family crests, profiles of their children or pets, golf motifs, college seals, Harley-Davidsons, their state, favorite sports teams, etc. Even if they own generic jewelry, men tend to wear pieces relating to their personal interests. Some of their jewelry might even be part of a collection. For example, a customer of one jeweler had a collection of more than one hundred watches.

Men usually prefer designs that are more angular, rather than curved, but there are exceptions. Generally, trade professionals recommend that men select sleek, bold designs instead of dainty ones. Keep in mind, your jewelry should make a positive statement about yourself.

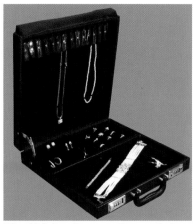

Fig. 16.1 Jewelry chest. *Cabinet and photo from A & A Jewelry Supply.*

Fig. 16.2 Jewelry case. *Case and photo from A & A Jewelry Supply.*

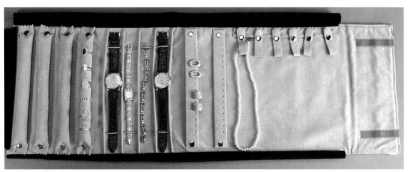

Fig. 16.3 Jewelry roll made of Italian suede. *Roll & photo from A & A Jewelry Supply.*

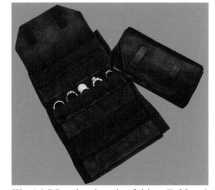

Fig. 16.4 Watch winder case. *Winder and photo from A & A Jewelry Supply.*

Fig.16.5 Leather jewelry folder. *Folder & photo from A & A Jewelry Supply.*

16

Caring for Your Jewelry

Which of the following scratches most easily?

♦ Glass
♦ Gold
♦ Platinum
♦ Turquoise

Pure gold scratches most easily because it's the softest. Glass and turquoise are harder than gold. They're even harder than platinum. This means that if you place jewelry in a box on top of other pieces, it could get scratched, especially by jewelry set with gemstones. Therefore, when you store jewelry, place each piece in a separate compartment, pouch or plastic bag, or wrap them individually in soft material. Padded jewelry bags with lots of pockets are also handy for storing jewelry.

The disadvantage of placing jewelry in cloth pouches or bags is that you can't see it and find it readily. One solution is to use stackable trays with or without compartments or large chests with trays or drawers (fig. 16.1). Jewelry cases, folding boxes, and rolls that open up with a large display area are also available (figures 16.2, 3, & 5). You can find these at jewelry supply stores for reasonable prices. It costs even less to place your jewelry separately in small clear plastic pouches and organize them in ordinary boxes. A word of caution about plastic—it may cause silver to tarnish more quickly.

Conventional jewelry boxes can protect pieces from damage if they're stored individually, but these types of boxes are one of the first places burglars look when they break into a house. Therefore, it's best to reserve jewelry boxes for costume jewelry when they're displayed on tables or dressers. Use your imagination to find a secure place in your house to hide jewelry pouches, rolls, cases and boxes. If expensive pieces are seldom worn, it may be wise to keep them in a safe deposit box.

Special storage boxes for watches called winders are popular with people who collect watches. These have computer controlled rotators, which keep the watches in good working condition (fig. 16.4). They are great gifts for watch connoisseurs.

Cleaning Metal Mountings

The safest way to clean jewelry mountings is to rub them with a soft cloth dipped in warm water containing a mild liquid detergent. Brushes and scouring pads can scratch metals such as gold, platinum and silver. Therefore, avoid using them to clean these metals, especially if the jewelry is plated. Powder cleansers and toothpaste can also wear away metal, so don't use them for cleaning jewelry.

Some jewelers like to clean jewelry with sudsy ammonia or window cleaner sprays. They're usually safe to *spray* on metal and most stones, but they may damage gems such as pearls, coral and turquoise. However, avoid soaking jewelry in ammonia. Overexposure to it can sometimes change or darken the color of certain solders or gemstones.

In the diamond trade, ethyl alcohol is frequently used to clean diamonds because it can dissolve grease build-up, and it evaporates quickly without leaving water spots. Avoid common isopropyl rubbing alcohol; it contains oils that can leave a film residue on your jewelry. Ethyl alcohol can be found in hardware stores, and it should only be used on stones that are not damaged by chemicals.

Removing tarnish, especially on silver, can be a challenge. One way of removing tarnish is to rub the silver with a soft, moist cloth and baking soda, which has a Mohs hardness value of 2.5. This value is about the same or less than that of silver alloys. Consequently, the soda is not as apt to wear away the silver as many other abrasives. In fact, baking soda is safe enough that many dentists recommend it as an ideal cleaning agent for teeth. Rinse the piece well with water so the baking soda does not remain in crevices. Another baking soda method, which does not wear away metal, is described on the following page.

Toothpaste and silver polish pastes can also remove tarnish, but the particles in them are usually harder than those of baking soda, making them more abrasive than baking soda. Silver polishes, however, may contain additional chemicals that make them more effective.

Removing Silver Tarnish

When silver is exposed to sulfur elements in the air, it tarnishes and forms silver sulfide, which is black. As a result, the silver is darkened. The silver can be returned to its former luster by removing the silver sulfide. There are two ways to remove it. One way is to remove the silver sulfide from the surface of the silver, but some silver will also be removed. The other way is to reverse the chemical reaction and turn silver sulfide back into silver. In this process, the silver remains in place.

Here's a simple way for you to conduct this electrolytic-type process, which will allow you to only remove the sulfate but leave the silver intact. You'll need a sheet of aluminum foil, hot water, baking soda, salt and a pot or pan. Then:

1) Line the pot or pan with the aluminum foil and place your tarnished silver jewelry item(s) or object(s) on top of the foil. **The object must have direct contact with the aluminum foil** for the process to work.

2) Pour hot water over the item so that it is entirely covered. Add a tablespoon of salt (two for a large pot) to create the electrolytic solution.

3) Pour a package of fresh (FRESH!) baking soda into the mix

4) Let it sit and watch how the sulfate is stripped off the silver surface. Remove the items when they are clean.

Naturally this process only works for silver items without pearls or other gems that should not be exposed to hot chemical solutions. Remember also that hot water can adversely affect the life span of glue.

This process works because aluminum has a greater affinity for sulfur than silver does. In the above process, the silver sulfide reacts with aluminum and sulfur atoms are transferred from silver to aluminum, freeing the silver metal and forming aluminum sulfide. Chemists represent this reaction with a chemical equation:

silver sulfide + aluminum = silver + aluminum sulfide

Silver alloys can differ in composition and may have tarnish layers other than silver sulfide. Consequently, the above method might not be adequate for removing all tarnishes from silver. Chemical shelf cleaners may be required, especially for silver that is below 925 in purity.

The above information is from Kathrin Schoenke, a jeweler and platinum industry consultant.

Liquid silver cleaners are also available, but they should not be used on jewelry set with stones such as pearls, coral, turquoise, malachite, etc. Read the labels on jewelry cleaners and polishes.

Silver can be restored to a perfect mirror polish by polishing it on a buffing wheel. Buffing removes the tarnish and little nicks and scratches that the piece might have sustained. Keep in mind that this process removes a small amount of silver, making it less suited for plated items.

Gold alloys often contain silver and copper. Since gold jewelry is normally made of alloyed gold rather than pure gold, it can also tarnish. The lower the karat value of the gold jewelry, the more likely it is to tarnish. Since jewelry gold is not pure, a variety of chemical products may discolor or dissolve it. A few of these products and their effect on gold and silver alloys are as follows:

♦ **Chlorine**—it can pit and dissolve the metal, causing prongs to snap and mountings to break apart. Solder connections are especially vulnerable. Afterwards, it might appear as if you've been sold defective or fake gold jewelry. Therefore, avoid wearing gold or silver jewelry in swimming pools or hot tubs that have chlorine disinfectants, and never soak it or clean it with bleach.

♦ **Lotions and cosmetics**—besides leaving a film on the jewelry piece, they may tarnish it, especially if it's made of 10K gold or silver. If possible, put your jewelry on last, after applying make-up and spraying your hair.

   Many cosmetics are composed of minerals that are actually harder than gold. When these minerals are rubbed against your gold jewelry, very small particles of gold are removed from the jewelry and deposited on your skin, causing dark stains. This phenomenon, called black dermographism, is explained in the October 10, 2000 issue of the *Journal of Chemical Education* by Barbara Kebbekus.

♦ **Perm solutions**—they have a tendency to turn 10K gold and low-karat solder joints dark brown or black.

♦ **Some medications**—they may cause a chemical reaction in certain people. This can make their skin turn black when it comes into contact with the gold alloy.

♦ **Polishing compounds**—they can blacken your skin if they remain on the metal. Polishing cloths sold in jewelry stores may contain a mild abrasive for shining the metal. When using these cloths, be sure to wash or wipe the metal thoroughly afterwards.

Cleaning Gemstones

If all gems were like diamonds, it would be easy to clean them. Untreated diamonds without bad fractures can be steam cleaned, boiled in acid, soaked in alcohol or vigorously vibrated in ultrasonic cleaners. These cleaning methods would ruin many other gems. Colored gems that have unusually good durability and resistance to damage from chemicals, heat and ultrasonic cleaning are:

♦ **Ruby and sapphire** that has not been dyed, oiled or fracture-filled

♦ **Spinel**

♦ **Alexandrite** and other chrysoberyls that haven't been fracture-filled

Any of the preceding gems, however, can be damaged by high heat and ultrasonic cleaning if the stone contains large fractures.

The safest way to clean a gemstone is to regularly wipe it with a soft cloth moistened with warm soapy water. Then dry it with a soft, lint-free cloth. Gems that aren't damaged by ammonia can be cleaned by spraying them with a window cleaner. If the dirt can't be washed off with a cloth, try using a toothpick or a Water Pik to remove it. If that doesn't work, have it professionally cleaned. Jewelers often clean stones with ultrasonic cleaners, which send high frequency sound waves through solutions. The vibrating fluid removes built-up dirt, but it can also shake poorly-set stones from their mountings and damage some types of gems.

Many gems are susceptible to damage or fading from strong heat and **thermal shock**—sudden temperature changes. These include:

♦ Amethyst
♦ Ammolite
♦ Apatite
♦ Calcite
♦ Emerald
♦ Fluorite
♦ Garnet
♦ Kunzite
♦ Lapis lazuli
♦ Larimar
♦ Opal
♦ Pearls
♦ Peridot
♦ Quartz
♦ Tanzanite
♦ Topaz
♦ Tourmaline
♦ Zircon

Fig. 16.6 Which of these stones is most durable—the blue tanzanites, the pink spinel or the orange spessartine garnet?

The pink spinel is the most resistant to scratching and breakage and can be safely cleaned in an ultrasonic. The tanzanites are the least resistant because of their lower hardness and their tendency to cleave if they are hit hard. The *GIA Gem Reference Guide* says to avoid cleaning tanzanite in ultrasonic cleaners. *Stones cut by Clay Zava; photo by Robert Weldon.*

You should not, for example, lie in the sun and then jump in a swimming pool while wearing these gems, nor should you go from a hot oven to a cold sink of water or from a hot tub to a cold shower. If you do, the sudden change of temperature could possibly cause the stones to crack or shatter. Heat can dry out stones like opal. Don't leave these gems sitting on a sunny window sill either. The heat can cause small cracks in some gems like malachite, opal, pearls and turquoise. It might make amethyst, kunzite and red tourmaline fade and it could dry out and discolor the fillings in emerald.

Coral, malachite, pearls and turquoise are very sensitive to chemicals. Ammonia and acid solutions as well as everyday products such as perfumes and lotions can harm them. Pickling solutions used by jewelers, and some acids, will etch the surface of peridot. Solvents such as alcohol and acetone will gradually dissolve the fillers in emeralds and other oiled or filled stones. Dyed lapis, dyed jade and other dyed stones are also adversely affected by solvents.

The following table indicates stones that should not be cleaned in ultrasonic cleaners. Most of the data in the chart is from the GIA *Gem Reference Guide*, an article by Deborah Martin in the summer 1987 issue of *Gems and Gemology* entitled "Gemstone Durability: Design to Display," and an article by Howard Rubin entitled "Jewelers' Guide to Gemstone Handling."

Gemstone	Ultrasonic Is it safe?	Comments
Aquamarine	Use caution	Avoid heat if liquid inclusions are present
Amber	Avoid	Avoid heat, acids and strong solvents
Ammonite	Avoid	Avoid heat, acids and solvents
Andalusite	Usually safe	Avoid heat if liquid inclusions are present
Apatite	Risky	May lose or change color if heated
Calcite	Avoid	Avoid heat and acids
Chalcedony	Use caution	Chemicals may attack dyed stones
Chrysoberyl	Usually safe	—
Coral	Risky	Avoid chemicals, especially acids
Cubic zirconia	Safe	Sensitive to high temperatures
Diamond	Usually safe	Ammonia, acids and repeated ultrasonic cleaning may damage some fracture fillings
Emerald	Avoid	Avoid heat and solvents like acetone and alcohol
Fluorite	Avoid	Avoid heat and sulfuric acid
Garnet	Use caution	Avoid thermal shock; ultrasonics are risky if liquid inclusions are present
Hematite	Safe	Avoid hydrochloric acid
Iolite	Risky	Avoid acids and thermal shock
Ivory	Avoid	Avoid heat and chemicals
Jade	Usually safe	Acids can affect polish on stones. Avoid solvents and ultrasonics if dyed.
Kunzite	Avoid	Avoid heat and strong light to prevent fading
Labradorite	Avoid	Avoid heat and acids
Lapis Lazuli	Avoid	Avoid acids, acetone and other solvents
Malachite	Avoid	Avoid chemicals and heat
Moonstone	Avoid	Avoid heat
Opal	Avoid	Avoid heat, thermal shock and alkalies

Gemstone	Ultrasonic?	Comments
Pearl	Avoid	Avoid heat & chemicals, especially acids
Peridot	Use caution	Avoid acids and pickling solutions
Quartz	Use caution	Avoid thermal shock
Transparent ruby and sapphire	Use caution	Chemicals and ultrasonics may damage dyed & oiled stones and some filled stones
Sodalite	Avoid	Avoid thermal shock
Star ruby and sapphire	Risky	Avoid ultrasonics with black star sapphires and with oiled or dyed stones
Spinel	Usually safe	—
Sunstone	Avoid	Avoid heat and acids
Tanzanite	Avoid	Avoid thermal shock
Topaz	Avoid	Avoid thermal shock
Tourmaline	Risky	Avoid thermal shock
Turquoise	Avoid	Avoid heat and chemicals
Zircon	Risky	Avoid thermal shock

Cleaning Pearls

Cleaning pearls is not complicated. After you wear them, just wipe them off with a soft cloth or chamois which can be dry or damp. This will prevent the dirt from accumulating and keep perspiration, which is slightly acidic, from eating away at the pearl nacre.

If the pearls have not been kept clean and are very dirty, they can be cleaned by your jeweler or they can be washed in water and a mild soap such as Ivory or Lux liquid (some liquid soaps damage pearls) and cleaned with a soft cloth. Pay attention to the areas around the drill holes where dirt may tend to collect. After washing them, lay the pearls flat in a moist kitchen towel to dry. After the towel is dry, they should be dry. Do not wear pearls when their string is wet. Wet strings stretch and attract dirt which is hard to remove. Likewise do not hang pearls to dry. As mentioned previously, do not clean pearls in ultrasonic cleaners or with steam cleaners, ammonia or acidic substances.

Miscellaneous Tips

♦ If possible, avoid wearing jewelry while participating in contact sports or doing housework, gardening, repairs, etc. The mounting can be damaged, and stones can be chipped, scratched and cracked. During rough work, if you want to wear a ring for sentimental reasons or to avoid losing it, wear protective gloves. Hopefully, your ring has a smooth setting style with no high prongs.

♦ When you place jewelry near a sink, make sure the drains are plugged or that it's put in a protective container. Otherwise, don't take the jewelry off.

♦ Clean your jewelry on a regular basis. Then you won't have to use risky procedures to clean it later on.

♦ Don't remove rings by pulling on any of their gemstones. Instead, grasp the metal ring portion. This will help prevent the stones from coming loose and getting dirty.

♦ Occasionally check your jewelry for loose stones. Shake it or tap it lightly with your forefinger while holding it next to your ear. If you hear the stones rattle or click, have a jeweler tighten the prongs.

♦ Avoid exposing your jewelry to sudden changes of temperature. If you wear it in a hot tub and then go in cold water with it on, the stones could crack or shatter. Also keep jewelry away from steam and hot pots and ovens in the kitchen.

♦ Take a photo of your jewelry (a macro lens is helpful). Just lay it all together on a table for the photo. If the jewelry is ever lost or stolen, you'll have documentation to help you remember and prove what you had. Expensive jewelry should be documented and appraised by a professional jewelry appraiser. You can find appraisal information in my *Gem & Jewelry Pocket Guide* and *Diamond Handbook*. My website **www.reneenewman.com** has a list of independent jewelry appraisers and appraisal organization links.

♦ About every six months, have a jewelry professional check your ring for loose stones or wear on the mounting. Many jewelers will do this free of charge, and they'll be happy to answer your questions regarding the care of your jewelry.

Suppliers of the Jewelry for Photos in This Book

Cover photo: Paula Crevoshay, www.crevoshay.com, Albuquerque, NM
Inside front cover photos
Top: Hubert Inc., www.hubertgem.com, Los Angeles, CA
Bottom: Zaffiro, www.zaffirojewelry.com, Portland, OR
Inside back cover photos
Top: Zaffiro, www.zaffirojewelry.com, Portland, OR
Bottom right: Divina Pearls, www.divinapearls.com, Santa Monica, CA
Bottom left: Abe Mor Diamond Cutters & Co, www.abemor.com , New York, NY
Half title page photo: Paula Crevoshay, www.crevoshay.com, Albuquerque, NM
Title page photo: Zaffiro, www.zaffirojewelry.com, Portland, OR
Photo facing title page: Hubert Inc., www.hubertgem.com, Los Angeles, CA

Chapter 1
Figs. 1.1, 3, 6-8 Sajen, Inc., www.sajenjewelry.com, Putney, VT
Fig. 1.2 Karen R. McGinn, Heritage Arts Lab, Woodstock, GA
Fig. 1.4 Bobby Mann, Temple Hills, MD
Fig. 1.5 K Brunini Jewels, www.kbrunini.com, Solana Beach, CA

Chapter 2
Fig. 2.1, 2 Pure Gold, El Sobrante, CA
Figs. 2.3, 11, 12 Varna Inc., www.varna.com, Los Angeles, CA
Fig. 2.4 GelinAbaci, Inc., www.gelinabaci.com, Los Angeles, CA
Figs. 2.17, 18 Joseph DuMouchelle Auctioneers, www.dumouchelleauction.com,
    Grosse Pointe Farms, MI
Fig. 2.18 Sweet Iron Silver Co., www.sweetiron.com, Didsbury, AB, Canada

Fig. 2.20 Dancing Designs, www.dancingdesignsjewelry.com,, Bethlehem, PA

Fig. 2.22 Art Carved and PAI, www.artcarvedbridal.com, New York, NY and www.luxurypalladium.com, Billings, MT

Fig. 2.23 Abe Mor Diamond Cutters & Co, www.abemor.com , New York, NY

Fig. 2.24 Mark B Mann, www.visualcominc.com & www.luxurypalladium.com, Billings, MT

Fig. 2.25 Mark Schneider, www.markschneiderdesign.com, Long Beach, CA

Figs. 2.26, 27, 28 The Bell Group, www.riogrande.com, Albuquerque, NM

Figs. 2.28, 29 Stuller, Inc. www.stuller.com, Lafayette, LA

Fig. 2,31 Heavy Stone Rings, www.heavystonerings.com, Orem, UT

Chapter 3

Fig. 3.1 Gemological Institute of America, www.gia.edu, Carlsbad, CA

Figs. 3.3, 4 Josam Diamond Trading Corp. , Los Angeles, CA

Figs. 3.8-13, 20, 28, 38 Zava Master Cuts, www.zavagems.com, Chapel Hill, NC

Fig. 3.17 J. Landau, Inc., www.landauideal.com, Los Angeles, CA

Fig. 3.18 Zaffiro, www.zaffirojewelry.com, Portland, OR

Fig. 3.19 Timeless Gem Designs, www.timelessgemdesigns.com, Los Angeles, CA

Fig. 3.21 Carolyn Tyler, www.carolyntyler.com, Santa Barbara, CA

Fig. 3.22 Todd Reed, Inc., www.toddreed.com, Boulder, CO

Fig. 3.23 Winc Creations, www.robertwander.com, Honolulu, Hawaii

Figs. 3.24-27, 29, 30 John Dyer / Precious Gemstones Co., www.finecolor.com Edina, MN

Fig. 3.31 Angela Conty, www.contydesigns.com, Schenectady, NY

Fig. 3.32, 36 Dancing Designs, www.dancingdesignsjewelry.com,, Bethlehem, PA

Figs. 3.33, 34 Fred & Kate Pearce, www.pearcejewelers.com, West Lebanon, NH

Fig. 3.35 Barbara Westwood, www.barbarawestwood.com Monument, CO

Fig. 3.37 Sherris Cottier Shank, www.gemscapes.com, Southfield, MI

Chapter 4

Fig. 4.1 Nerses Yahiayan, Los Angeles, CA

Fig. 4.2 Stamper Black Hills Gold Jewelry, www.stamperbhg.com, Rapid City, SD

Figs. 4.3-5, 15-19 Mark B Mann, Palladium Alliance International (PAI) www.visualcominc.com, www.luxurypalladium.com, Billings, MT

Figs. 4.6 & 4.7 Peggy Croft Wax Sculpting, Los Angeles, CA

Figs. 4.8 to 4.11 Varna, www.varna.com, Los Angeles, CA

Fig. 4.12 LRG Studio 13, Inc., Los Angeles, CA

Fig. 4.13 True Knots, www.trueknots.com, Los Angeles, CA

Fig. 4.14 Stuller, Inc. www.stuller.com, Lafayette, LA

Fig. 4.20 Oliver & Espig Jewelers, Santa Barbara, CA

Figs. 4.21, 22 Revere Academy of Jewelry Arts, www.revereacademy.com, San Francisco, CA

Fig. 4.23 The Roxx Limited, Baltimore, MD

Chapter 5

Fig. 5.1 Rubin & Son, www.rubin-and-son.com, Antwerp, Belgium

Figs. 5.5, 9, 12, 13, Varna, www.varna.com, Los Angeles, CA

Fig. 5.8 J. Landau, Inc, www.landauideal.com, Los Angeles, CA

Fig. 5.10 Hubert, Inc., www.hubertgem.com, Los Angeles, CA

Fig. 5.11 Sugarman-Frantz Designs, www.sugarmandesigns.com, Santa Fe, NM

Fig. 5.14 Todd Reed, Inc., www.toddreed.com, Boulder, CO

Figs. 5.15, 16, 17, 18, 21 Stuller, Inc., www.stuller.com, Lafayette, LA

Fig. 5.19 King Plutarco, Inc, www.kingplutarco.com, Los Angeles, CA

Fig. 5.20 Mark Schneider, www.markschneiderdesign.com, Long Beach, CA

Chapter 6

Figs. 6.4, 6, 8, 9, 10 True Knots Co, www.trueknots.com, Los Angeles, CA

Fig. 6.2 Aaron Henry Designs, www.aaronhenry.com, Los Angeles, CA

Fig. 6.5 Peggy Croft Wax Sculpting, Los Angeles, CA

Fig. 6.7 The Bell Group, www.riogrande.com, Albuquerque, NM

Figs. 6.11, 27 Gary Dulac Goldsmith, Vero Beach, Fl

Fig. 6.12 Oliver & Espig Jewelers, Santa Barbara, CA

Fig. 6.13 Joseph DuMouchelle Auctioneers, www.dumouchelleauction.com, Grosse Pointe Farms, MI

Fig. 6.14 GelinAbaci, Inc., www.gelinabaci.com, Los Angeles, CA

Fig. 6.16 JFF Jewelry Supply, Doraville (Atlanta), GA

Fig. 6.17 Divina Pearls, www.divinapearls.com, Santa Monica, CA

Fig. 6.18 Zaffiro, www.zaffirojewelry.com, Portland, OR

Fig. 6.19-23 Mark B Mann, www.visualcominc.com, Billings, MT

Fig. 6.24 Varna, www.varna.com, Los Angeles, CA

Fig. 6.25 Designed by Alan Hodgkinson, made by Bert McCrum, Glasgow, Scotland

Fig. 6.28 Hubert, Inc., www.hubertgem.com, Los Angeles, CA

Figs. 6.29, 32 Mahlia Collection, www.mahliacollection.com, Tucson, AZ

Fig. 6.31 George Sawyer, www.georgesawyer.com, Minneapolis, MN

Figs. 6.35, 36 Forest Jewelers, www.forestjewelers.com, Princeton, NJ

Fig. 6.38 Tempus Gems, www.tempusgems.com, New Delhi, India

Chapter 8

Figs. 8.1-3, 7 A & Z Pearls, www.azpearls.com, Los Angeles, CA

Fig. 8.4 Mahlia Collection, www.mahliacollection.com, Tucson, AZ

Fig. 8.5 Abe Mor Diamond Cutters & Co, www.abemor.com , New York, NY

Fig. 8.6 Zaffiro, www.zaffirojewelry.com, Portland, OR

Fig. 8.7 King Plutarco, Inc, www.kingplutarco.com, Los Angeles, CA

Chapter 9

Figs. 9.1, 7, 8, 22 Benjamin & Co, www.benjamincompany.com, Los Angeles

Figs. 9.2– 4, 11, 13, 18, 23 Media Imports, www.mediaimports.com, Los Angeles

Figs. 9.5, 6, 20, 22, 24, 26, 33, 35, 38–44, 46–49 Stuller, Inc. www.stuller.com, Lafayette, LA

Fig. 9.9 Hallock Jewelry, www.hallockjewelry.com, Anaheim, CA

Figs. 9.15, 16 H. S. Walsh & Sons Ltd., www.hswalsh.com, Beckenham, UK

Figs. 9.17, 25, Aurora Imports, www.auroraimports.com, Los Angeles, CA

Fig. 9.27 Christian Tse, www.christiantse.com, Pasadena, CA

Fig. 9-28 Barbara Westwood, www.barbarawestwood.com Monument, CO

Fig. 9.29 Winc Creations, www.robertwander.com, Honolulu, Hawaii

Fig. 9.30 Christopher's Fine Jewelry, www.christophers-finejewelry.com, Champaign., IL

Fig. 9.45 Mahlia Collection, www.mahliacollection.com, Tucson, AZ

Chapter 10

Figs. 10.1, 19 The Bell Group, www.riogrande.com, Albuquerque, NM

Figs. 10.2-13, 18, 20 Stuller, Inc., www.stuller.com, Lafayette, LA

Fig. 10.14 Eve J Alfillé Gallery & Studio, www.evejewelry.com, Evanston, IL

Fig. 10.15 Grobet USA, www.grobetusa.com, Carlstadt, NJ

Fig. 10.16 Jemco Jewelry Supply, www.jemco-usa.com, Houston, TX.

Fig. 10-17 FDJ On Time LLC, www.fdjtool.com, Winter Park, FL

Chapter 11

Figs. 11.1, 2, 15-28 Stuller, Inc., www.stuller.com, Lafayette, LA

Figs. 11.6 & 7 HOOKer Earrings, www.hooker-earrings.com, Laguna Beach, CA

Figs. 11.8-13 King Plutarco, www.kingplutarco.com, Los Angeles, CA

Fig. 11.14 A & Z Pearls, www.azpearls.com, Los Angeles, CA

Chapter 12

Fig. 12.1 Stuller, Inc., www.stuller.com, Lafayette, LA

Figs. 12.2-5 Todd Reed, Inc., www.toddreed.com, Boulder, CO

Fig. 12.6 Sajen, Inc., www.sajenjewelry.com, Putney, VT

Figs. 12.7, 10 FDJ On Time LLC, www.fdjtool.com, Winter Park, FL

Fig. 12.8 The Bell Group, www.riogrande.com, Albuquerque, NM

Fig. 12.9 King Plutarco, www.kingplutarco.com, Los Angeles, CA

Chapter 13

Figs. 13.1, 2, 7, 8, 13-15, 18 Joseph DuMouchelle Auctioneers, Gross Pointe Farms, MI, www.dumouchelleauction.com,

Figs. 13.3-6, 10-12 Karen R. McGinn, Heritage Arts Lab, Woodstock, GA

Fig. 13.9, 17 Timeless Gem Designs, www.timelessgemdesigns.com, Los Angeles

Fig. 13.16 Sajen, Inc., www.sajenjewelry.com, Putney, VT

Chapter 14

Figs. 14.1-3, 18-22 A & Z Pearls, www.azpearls.com, Los Angeles, CA

Figs. 14.4, 5 Timeless Gem Designs, www.timelessgemdesigns.com, Los Angeles

Suppliers of the Jewelry for Photos in This Book

Figs. 14.6, 7 .Hooker Earrings, www.hooker-earrings.com, Laguna Beach, CA
Fig. 14.8 King Plutarco, Inc., www.kingplutarco.com, Los Angeles, CA
Fgs. 14.9, 10   Sajen, Inc., www.sajenjewelry.com, Putney, VT
Figs. 14.11-14 Joseph DuMouchelle Auctioneers, www.dumouchelleauction.com,
    Grosse Pointe Farms, MI
Figs. 14.16, 17 Carolyn Tyler, www.carolyntyler.com, Santa Barbara, CA
Figs. 14.26-27 Todd Reed, Inc., www.toddreed.com, Boulder, CO

Chapter 15
Figs. 15.1, 7 The Bell Group, www.riogrande.com, Albuquerque, NM
Figs. 15.2, 3, 8 Mark Schneider, www.markschneiderdesign.com, Long Beach, CA
Figs. 15.4, 9 Timeless Gem Designs, www.timelessgemdesigns.com, Los Angeles
Fig. 15.5 Stuller, Inc., www.stuller.com, Lafayette, LA
Fig. 15.6 Joseph DuMouchelle Auctioneers, www.dumouchelleauction.com,
    Grosse Pointe Farms, MI

Chapter 16
Figs. 16.1-5 A & A Jewelry Supplies, www.aajewelry.com, Los Angeles, CA
Fig. 16.6 Zava Master Cuts, www.zavagems.com, Chapel Hill, NC

Bibliography

Books

Allen, Gina. *Gold!* New York: Thomas Y. Crowell, 1964.

Arbetter, Lisa. *Secrets of Style: The Complete Guide to Dressing your Best Every Day.* New York: In Style Books, Time Inc. 2005.

Avery, James. *The Right Jewelry for You.* Austin, TX: Eakin Press, 1988.

Bovin, Murray. *Jewelry Making.* Forest Hills, NY: Bovin Publishing, 1967.

Branson, Oscar T. *What You Need to Know About Your Gold and Silver.* Tucson, AZ: Treasure Chest Publications, 1980.

Brod, I. Jack. *Consumer's Guide to Buying and Selling Gold, Silver, and Diamonds.* Garden City, NY: Doubleday, 1985.

Burkett, Russell. *Everything You Wanted to Know about Gold and Other Precious Metals.* Whittier, CA: Gem Guides Book Co., 1975.

Carroll, Julia. *Collecting Costume Jewelry 101.* Paducah, KY: Collector Books, 2006.

Cavelti, Peter C. *New Profits in Gold, Silver & Strategic Metals.* New York: McGraw-Hill, 1985.

Dariaux, Genevieve Antoine. *A Guide to Elegance.* New York: William Morrow, 2004.

Edwards, Rod. *The Technique of Jewelry.* New York: Charles Scribner's Sons, 1977.

Farr, Kendall. *The Pocket Stylist: Behind the Scenes Expertise from a Fashion Pro on Creating Your Own Unique Look.* New York: Gotham Books, 2004.

Gemological Institute of America. *Appraisal Seminar handbook.*
Gemological Institute of America. *Gold & Precious Metals Course.*
Gemological Institute of America. *Jewelry Repair Workbook.*
Gemological Institute of America. *Jewelry Sales Course.*
Gemological Institute of America. *Jewelry Essentials*

Goldemberg, Rose Leiman. *Antique Jewelry: a Practical and Passionate Guide.* New York: Crown Publishing Co., 1976.

Green, Timothy. *The Gold Companion*. London: Rosendale Press, 1991.

Gould, Maurice M. *Gould's Gold and Silver Guide to Coins*.

Hall, Judy. *The Crystal Bible*. Cincinnati. OH, Walking Stick Press, 2004.

Hemingway, Patricia Drake. *The Well-dressed Woman: A Complete Guide to Creating the Right Look for Yourself and Your Career*. New York: New American Library, 1977.

Howard, Margaret Ann. *Decorate Me Gorgeous*. Oklahoma, City: Margaret Howard.1984.

Kelly, Clinton and Stacy London. *Dress Your Best: The Complete Guide to Finding the Style That's Right for Your Body*. New York: Three Rivers Press. 2005.

Jarvis, Charles A. *Jewelry Manufacture and Repair*. New York: Bonanza, 1979.

Marcum, David. *Fine Gems and Jewelry*. Homewood, IL.: Dow Jones-Irwin, 1986.

Mathis, Carla Mason, Connor, Helen Villa. *The Triumph of Individual Style*. Timeless Editions, 1993.

McCreight, Tim. *The Complete Metalsmith: An Illustrated Handbook*. Worcester, MA: Davis Publications, 1991.

McCreight, Tim. *Jewelry: Fundamentals of Metalsmithing*. Madison, WI: Hand Books Press, 1997.

McCreight, Tim (editor). *Metals Technic*. Cape Elisabeth, Maine: Brynmorgan Press. 1992.

McGrath, Jinks. *The Encyclopedia of Jewelry Making Techniques*. Philadelphia: Running Press, 1995.

Merton, Henry A. *Your Gold & Silver*. New York: Macmillan, 1981.

Miller, Anna M. *Gems and Jewelry Appraising*. New York: Van Nostrand Reinhold, 1988.

Miller, Anna M. *Illustrated Guide to Jewelry Appraising*. New York: Van Nostrand Reinhold, 1990.

Miller, Judith. *Costume Jewelry: The Complete Visual Reference and Price Guide:* London, 2003.

Miguel, Jorge. *Jewelry: How to Create Your Image*. Dallas: Taylor Publishing Co. 1986.

Morton, Philip. *Contemporary Jewelry*. New York: Holt, Rinehart, and Winston, 1976.

Newman, Renée, *Diamond Ring Buying Guide*. Los Angeles: International Jewelry Publications, 2005.

Newman, Renée, *Gem & Jewelry Pocket Guide*. Los Angeles, International Jewelry Publications, 2006.

170

Newman, Renée, *Gold & Platinum Jewelry Buying Guide.* Los Angeles: International Jewelry Publications, 2000.

Ostier, Marianne. *Jewels and the Woman: The Romance, Magic, and Art of Feminine Adornment.* New York: Horizong Press, 1958.

Peschek-Bohmer, Flora, Schreiber, Gisela. *Healing Crystals and Gemstones From Amethyst to Zircon.* Old Saybrook, CT. Konecky & Konecky, 2003.

Pitman, Ann Mitchell. *Inside the Jewelry Box. A Collector's Guide to Costume Jewelry.* Paducah, KY: Collector Books, 2004.

Penny Proddow, Marion Fasel. *With This Ring: The Ultimate Guide to Wedding Jewelry.* New York: Bulfinch, Press, 2004.

Revere, Alan, *Professional Goldsmithing.* New York: Van Nostrand Reinhold, 1991.

Richards, Alison. *Handmade Jewelry.* New York: Funk & Wagnalls. 1976.

Ruhle-Diebener-Verlag. *Practical Platinumsmith: 3rd Edition.* Stuttgart: Ruhle-Diebener-Verlag, 1995.

Sarett, Morton R. *The Jewelry in Your Life.* Chicago: Nelson-Hall, 1979.

Schumann, Walter. *Gemstones of the World.* New York: Sterling 1997.

Simmons, Robert & Ahsian, Naisha. *Book of Stones. Who They Are and What They Teach.* East Montpellier, VT, 2005.

Smith, Ernest. *Working in Precious Metals.* Colchester, England: N. A. G. Press Ltd. 1933.

Sprintzen, Alice. *Jewelry: Basic Techniques and Design.* Radnor, PA: Chilton, 1980

Sutherland, C. H. V. *Gold: Its Beauty, Power and Allure.* New York: McGraw-Hill, 1969.

Untracht, Oppi. *Jewelry Concepts & Technology.* New York: Doubleday, 1982.

Von Neumann, Robert. *The Design and Creation of Jewelry.* Radnor, PA: Chilton, 1972.

Woodall, Trinny and Constantine, Susannah. Trinny and Susannah, *What you Wear can Change Your Life.* New York: Riverhead Books, 2004.

Magazines

American Jewelry Manufacturer. Philadelphia, PA

Canadian Jeweler. Toronto, ON, Style Communications Inc.

Gems and Gemology. Carlsbad, CA: Gemological Institute of America.

Jewelers Circular Keystone. New York, NY, Reed Business Information

Lapidary Journal. Loveland, CO, Interweave Press LLC.

MJSA Journal. Providence, RI, Manufacturing Jewelers & Suppliers of America

Modern Jeweler. Melville, NY, Cygnus Publishing

National Jeweler. New York, NY, VNU Business Publications

Professional Jeweler. Philadelphia, PA: Bond Communications

Miscellaneous (Articles, Catalogues, Brochures, etc.)
A & A Jewelry Supply Catalogue.

Consumer and Corporate Affairs Canada. "A Guide to the Precious Metals Marking Act and Regulations."

Federman, David. "Electroforming: Big, bold and light." Modern Jeweler, p. 65-66, January, 1993.

GIA and the World Gold Council. The Gold Seminar Handbook.

Johnson Matthey, "Platinum Jewelry Products."

Mercer, Meredith E. "Methods for Determining the Gold Content of Jewelry Metals." Gems & Gemology, p. 222-233, Winter 1992.

Platinum Guild International. "Talking Platinum."

"Platinum Alloys and Their Application in Jewelry Making" by the Platinum Guild International USA, written by Jurgen Maerz, Director of Technical Education with assistance from Taryn Biggs & Stefanie Taylor of Mintek, South Africa, Johnson Matthey, Engelhard-Clal, Imperial Smelting, C. Hafner Co. and Techform LLC. 1999.

Reactive Metals Studio Inc. 1993 Catalogue. Clarkdale, Az.

Rio Grande *Gems & Findings* Catalogue.

Rubin & Son. *Supplies and Equipment for the Jewelry-Diamond Trade, Gemological Instruments.*

Stuller. *The Findings Book.*

Stuller. *The Finished Jewelry Book.*

Stuller. *The Mountings Book.*

Swest Inc. *Jewelers' Findings & Stones & Metals.*

Index

adjustable ring shank 118, 119
alloy 7
anchor chain 97
anniversary stones 42, 43
anticlastic raising 69, 70
antique jewelry 3, 136
artisan jewelry 4
avoirdupois weight 16

baguette 32, 115
bangle 128, 129, 131
bar setting 63, 64, 113
barrel clasp 105
base metal 10
bead chain 91, 100
bead setting 62, 64, 66
beads 2, 36, 37, 101, 103
bezel facet 30
bezel setting 62, 113
bib necklace 84
birthstones 29, 42, 43
Bismarck chain 98
body jewelry 4
box chain 97, 98
box clasp 104, 105
bracelet sizer 130, 131
bracelets 25, 127-131, 142, 151
braiding 71, 72
brass 10, 26

bright polish 52, 67, 99
brilliant Cut 30-32, 34, 35
briolettes 34
bronze 10
brooch 2, 36, 55, 74, 133-139
brushed finish 67
button earrings 124-126

cable chain 96, 98
cabochon 31, 32, 35
carat 8, 14, 16, 33
caring for your jewelry 153-161
casting 45-50, 52, 60, 73, 78
Ceylon cut 34
chain lengths 92
chains 91-103
channel setting 62-64, 113
charm bracelet 128, 130
chasing 71, 75, 76
choker 83, 84, 87, 144
choosing flattering jewelry 79-82
clasps 103-108, 133, 144
claw setting 57
cleaning and care 154-161
    gemstones 157-161
    metal mountings 154-156
clips 133-137, 139, 143
clip-on earrings 120
cluster earrings 124, 125, 136

collectible jewelry 3
Comfort Fit ring 111
costume jewelry 3, 4, 137, 146, 153
critical angle 29
crown 29, 30, 32-34, 69
crystals 32, 38, 102
cuff 19, 25, 128-130, 139, 150
culet 29, 30, 32
curb link chain 97
custom jewelry 3
cutting style 30-32

dangle 84, 124-126, 136
decorative techniques 69-77
designer jewelry 3, 4
diamond-cut 94, 99, 100
die-striking 45, 49, 99
die-struck 21, 54, 55
dog collar 84, 87

earrings 2, 34, 50-53, 63, 75, 81, 120-126, 140, 142
electroforming 45, 51
electroplating 10, 51
embossing 71, 72
emerald cut 31, 32
enameling 71, 72, 78
engraving 48-51, 71-73
estate jewelry 3, 136
etching 71

face shapes 79, 126
facets 29-34, 36, 39
fake gold 13, 156
fancy chain 91, 99
figaro 91, 97
filigree 71, 72
findings 16
fine gold 3, 8, 14

fine jewelry 2-4, 18
fineness 8, 9, 11, 13, 15, 18, 20
Finger Fit® 119
finger gauge 118
finish 67-78
fish-hook clasp 105
flat chain 91, 95
flexible bracelet 128-130
florentine finish 67, 68
foldover clasp 107
fusion 71, 74, 75

gemstone cutting 33
gemstone basic facts 29-44
GIA 133, 158
girdle 29, 30, 32, 58, 59, 62, 65
glassbeaded finish 67-69, 78
gold 2-4, 7-18, 21, 23-26, 153, 154, 156
    alloy 8, 156
    alloys 17, 23, 74, 156
gold filled 11
gold flashed 10
gold overlay 12
gold plate 12
grain 14, 74
gram 14, 16, 51, 93, 94, 99, 100
granulation 35, 72, 74, 76
Gucci chain 97

hallmark 11, 14, 15
hammered finish 68-70
hand fabrication 45, 52
handmade jewelry 54
hand-fabricated 48, 52-56
hand-fabricated ring 48
head 55, 60
heart shape 126
herringbone chain 95, 96, 98
hidden bead clasp 108

hollow rings 112
hollow rope chain 93
hook clasps 106
HOOKer Earrings 120, 142
hook-ons 121
hoop earrings 124, 125

iridium 7, 10, 12

jewelry
    care and cleaning 153-161
    classifications 2-6
    finishes 67-78
    flattering 79-82
    manufacturing methods 45-56
    men's 148-151
    metals information 7-28
    settings 57-66
    storage 152-154
    tips for men 148-151
    versatile 139-147
judging finish 77, 78

karat 8, 9, 11, 15, 18
    (Carat) 8
    gold 8, 9, 11, 18, 35
    value 156
kisses and hugs chain 91, 105

lariat 84-86
link chain 91, 93, 95-99, 148
lobster clasp 104, 105
lobster claw 104
lost wax casting 45-48
loupe 57, 58

macles 38, 129
magnetic clasp 105
manufacturing methods 45-56
marquise 30, 39

matinee 84, 85
matte finish 67, 69, 148
microwire 100
milgraining 74, 75
mixed cut 34
mokume gane 74, 76
mounting 16, 57, 58, 110, 111, 154
mystery clasp 107, 144

neck wires 100
necklaces 83-90, 100-103
neckpiece 102
nickel 7, 10, 17, 20, 23, 26
non-traditional cuts 39-41

omega chain 96
omega clip 122, 123
opera length 84
osmium 10, 12
oxidizing 74

palladium 21-23, 47, 53, 73, 74
partial bezel 61, 62
pavé setting 64, 65
pavilion 29, 30, 32
pear shape 143
pearls 84, 85, 87-89, 123, 124, 140, 144, 145, 160
pennyweight 14, 16
pewter 12
pierced earrings 121-124
pins 133-139, 143, 149, 151
PLAT 9, 10, 13, 15, 20
platinum alloys 7, 14, 26
platinum content 7, 9, 10
platinum group metals 10, 12, 21
plumb gold 8, 11, 94
precious metals 12, 14, 21, 26
prong setting 57-61, 113

PT 9, 10, 20
pure gold 8, 16-18, 21, 153, 156
push clasp 104, 105
quality mark 15

radiant cut 31
refining 17, 24
repoussé 76
reticulation 75, 76
rhodium 10, 12, 20, 23, 24, 28
ring 109-120
    guard 117, 118
    practical tips 110-117
    size 115-119
    stretcher 117, 118
riviere 84, 86
roll printing 75
rolled gold plate 12
roller printing 76
rope chain 55, 92, 93, 99
rough 29, 33, 38
rubber mold 45, 46, 56
ruthenium 7, 8, 10, 12, 23

San Marco chain 91, 99
sandblasted finish 69, 70
satin finish 69
sautoir 84
screw clasp 107
screw-back earrings 120
seat 58-60
selecting bracelets 127, 128
selecting earrings 121, 124
selecting necklaces 83
serpentine chain 96
setting 17, 57-66, 112, 113, 149, 161
setting styles 57- 66
shank 17, 55, 60, 63, 112, 114, 118, 119, 149

silver 3, 12-14, 16-21, 129, 130, 137, 142, 147, 150, 153-156
silver jewelry 18-21, 82, 155, 156
silver tarnish 20, 155
Singapore chain 97
single cut 34
slide clasp 107
snake chain 91, 99, 100
solder 17, 74, 77, 94, 156
soldering 17, 52, 53, 71
solid gold 9, 45
specific gravity 21, 24, 26, 28
spring ring 104
stainless steel 25, 26, 100, 101, 104, 151
stampato 99
stamping 45, 49, 50, 76, 99
station bracelet 128
station necklace 87
step cut 31, 32, 34
sterling silver 13, 14, 18-20, 25, 57, 105, 129, 130, 147, 150
stippling 76
straight-line necklace 84
stud earrings 120

table 29, 30
table cut 32
tael 15
titanium 12, 21, 24-26, 28, 112, 115, 117, 148, 151
toggle clasp 105
torsade 87, 88
trademark 11, 15, 97
troy ounce 14, 16
tube clasp 107
tungsten 12, 21, 25-28, 117, 151

ultrasonic 157-160

vermeil 2, 14

weight conversion 16
welding 17
white gold 17, 18, 21, 23, 24, 64,
        82, 100, 136, 138

Other Books by RENÉE NEWMAN
Graduate Gemologist (GIA)

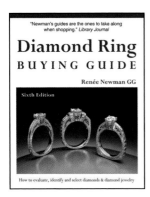

"Newman's guides are the ones to take along when shopping." *Library Journal*

Diamond Ring
BUYING GUIDE

Renée Newman GG

Sixth Edition

How to evaluate, identify and select diamonds & diamond jewelry

Diamond Ring Buying Guide
How to Evaluate, Identify and Select
Diamonds & Diamond Jewelry

"**An entire course on judging diamonds in 156 pages of well-organized information.** . . . The photos are excellent . . . Clear and concise, it serves as a check-list for the purchase and mounting of a diamond . . . another fine update in a series of books that are useful to both the jewelry industry and consumers."
Gems & Gemology

"**A wealth of information** . . . delves into the intricacies of shape, carat weight, color, clarity, setting style, and cut—happily avoiding all industry jargon and keeping explanations streamlined enough so even the first-time diamond buyer can confidently choose a gem."
Booklist

"Succinctly written in a step-by-step, outlined format with plenty of photographs to illustrate the salient points; it could help keep a lot of people out of trouble. Essentially, it is a **fact-filled text devoid of a lot of technical mumbo-jumbo.** This is a definite thumbs up!"
C. R. Beesley, President, American Gemological Laboratories

156 pages, 193 color & b/w photos, 7" X 9", ISBN 0-929975-32-4, US$17.95

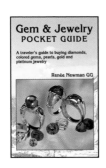

Gem & Jewelry
POCKET GUIDE

A traveler's guide to buying diamonds, colored gems, pearls, gold and platinum jewelry

Renée Newman GG

Gem & Jewelry Pocket Guide
Small enough to use while shopping locally or abroad

"**Brilliantly planned, painstakingly researched, and beautifully produced** . . . this handy little book comes closer to covering all of the important bases than any similar guides have managed to do. From good descriptions of the most popular gem materials (plus gold and platinum), to jewelry craftsmanship, treatments, gem sources, appraisals, documentation, and even information about U.S. customs for foreign travelers—it is all here. I heartily endorse this wonderful pocket guide."
John S. White, former Curator of Gems & Minerals at the Smithsonian,
Lapidary Journal

"**Short guides don't come better than this.** . . . As always with this author, the presentation is immaculate and each opening displays high-class pictures of gemstones and jewellery."
Journal of Gemmology

156 pages, 108 color photos, 4½" by 7", ISBN 0-929975-30-8, US$11.95

Available at major bookstores and jewelry supply stores

For more information, see **www.reneenewman.com**

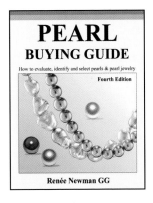

Pearl Buying Guide

How to Evaluate, Identify, Select and Care for Pearls & Pearl Jewelry

"**Copious color photographs** . . . explains how to appraise and distinguish among all varieties of pearls . . . takes potential buyers and collectors through the ins and outs of the pearl world. *Publisher's Weekly*

"**An indispensable guide** to judging [pearl] characteristics, distinguishing genuine from imitation, and making wise choices . . . useful to all types of readers, from the professional jeweler to the average patron . . . **highly recommended.**" *Library Journal*

"A **well written, beautifully illustrated** book designed to help retail customers, jewelry designers, and store buyers make informed buying decisions about the various types of pearls and pearl jewelry. The photos are abundant and well chosen, and the use of a coated stock contributes to the exceptional quality of the reproduction. Consumers also will find this book a source of accurate and easy-to-understand information about a topic that has become increasingly complex."

Gems & Gemology

156 pages, 208 color & b/w photos, 7" by 9", ISBN 0-929975-35-9, US$19.95

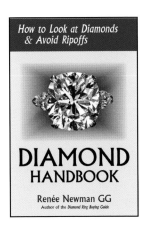

Diamond Handbook

How to Look at Diamonds & Avoid Ripoffs

Provides additional details and photos on clarity & cut, and covers topics not included in the *Diamond Ring Buying Guide* such as:

◆ Antique diamonds and jewelry
◆ Branded diamonds
◆ Diamond certificates, reports, and appraisals
◆ Diamond recutting
◆ Diamond types and synthetic diamonds
◆ Choosing a jeweler, appraiser, and gem lab

"The text covers everything the buyer needs to know, with useful comments on lighting and first-class black and white images that show up features better than those in colour. No other text in current circulation discusses recutting and its possible effects, and the author's discussion of the new topic of branded diamonds conveniently brings together a number of examples of particular cuts peculiar to different firms. . . . Brief and useful notes describe the present position of synthetic gem diamond and treated diamond. Rip-offs are soberly described and sensation avoided. **This is a must for anyone buying, testing or valuing a polished diamond and for students in many fields.**" *Journal of Gemmology*

186 pages, 7 color and 242 b/w photos, 6" x 9", US$18.95
Available at major bookstores and jewelry supply stores

Other Books by RENÉE NEWMAN

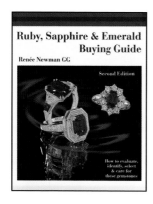

Ruby, Sapphire & Emerald Buying Guide

How to evaluate, identify, and select these gemstones

"**Enjoyable reading . . . profusely illustrated with color photographs** showing not only the beauty of finished jewelry but close-ups and magnification of details such as finish, flaws and fakes . . . Sophisticated enough for professionals to use . . . highly recommended . . . **Newman's guides are the ones to take along when shopping.**" *Library Journal*

"**Solid, informative and comprehensive** . . . dissects each aspect of ruby and sapphire value in detail . . . a wealth of grading information . . . a definite thumbs-up. There is something here for everyone."
C. R. Beesley, President, American Gemological Laboratories, *JCK Magazine*

"**The best produced book on gemstones I have yet seen in this price range** (how is it done?). This is the book for anyone who buys, sells or studies gemstones. This style of book (and similar ones by the same author) is the only one I know which introduces actual trade conditions and successfully combines a good deal of gemmology with them . . . **Buy it, read it, keep it.**"
Michael O'Donoghue, *Journal of Gemmology*

164 pages, 178 color & 21 b/w photos, 7" by 9", US$19.95

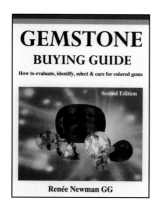

Gemstone Buying Guide

How to Evaluate, Identify and Select
Colored Gems

"Praiseworthy, **a beautiful gem-pictorial reference** and a help to everyone in viewing colored stones as a gemologist or gem dealer would. . . . One of the finest collections of gem photographs I've ever seen . . . If you see the book, you will probably purchase it on the spot." *Anglic Gemcutter*

"**A quality Buying Guide** that is recommended for purchase to consumers, gemologists and students of gemmology—irrespective of their standard of knowledge of gemmology. The information is comprehensive, factual, and well presented. Particularly noteworthy in this book are the quality colour photographs that have been carefully chosen to illustrate the text." *Australian Gemmologist*

"**Beautifully produced.** . . . With colour on almost every opening few could resist this book whether or not they were in the gem and jewellery trade.
Journal of Gemmology

156 pages, 281 color photos, 7" X 9", ISBN 0-929975-34-0, US$19.95

Osteoporosis Prevention

A *Proactive* Approach to Strong Bones and Good Health

RENÉE NEWMAN

"A competent and thoroughly "reader friendly" approach to preventing osteoporosis. Inclusive of information on how to: help prevent osteoporosis and broken bones; get enough calcium and other bone nutrients from food; make exercise safe and fun; retain a youthful posture; select a bone density center; get maximum benefit from your bone density exam; understand bone density reports; help seniors maintain their muscles and their bones; how medical professionals can motivate patients; and how to be a savvy patient. *Osteoporosis Prevention* should be a part of every community health center and public library Health & Medicine reference collection for non-specialist general readers."

Midwest Book Review

"I was impressed with the comprehensive nature of *Osteoporosis Prevention* and its use of scientific sources. The fact that the author has struggled with bone loss and can talk from personal experience makes the book more interesting and easy to read. Another good feature is that the book has informative illustrations and tables, which help clarify important points. I congratulate the author for writing a sound and thorough guide to osteoporosis prevention."

Ronald Lawrence, MD, PhD
Co-chair of the first Symposium on Osteoporosis of the National Institute on Aging

"A wonderful, wonderful book! Anybody concerned about osteoporosis should definitely read it." Frankie Boyer, host of the nationally syndicated Frankie Boyer Show

"I really liked the personalized examples in this book and the overall depth of information. I learned things I'd never known before. For example, I didn't realize how many different diseases and drugs could lead to osteoporosis. . . . I learned a great deal about bone density reports and testing. *Osteoporosis Prevention* has a very user-friendly layout and writing style, which makes it easy to read. I've given copies of it to my sister, a couple of friends, and I've mentioned it to some of my patients. It has a lot of beneficial advice on diet, exercise, supplements and posture. I highly recommend this book to anybody who wants a good overview of osteoporosis prevention." Cathy Davis, orthopedic RN

"I very much enjoyed reading *Osteoporosis Prevention*. I felt like I was on an educational adventure into the world of DXA tests and bone health. Rather than being very stiff and dryly educational, I found the reading to be captivating, with warmth and personal enthusiasm. Recently entering the world of menopause myself, I was delighted to find a book that encouraged me to be proactive about my bone health, even if my medical insurance won't pay for a DXA test yet. On a professional level as an RN on an ortho-neuro floor, I get to see first hand the problems that osteoporosis can contribute to with spine and bone fractures. It slows the healing process and tarnishes the golden years. Proactive prevention is definitely the way to go and this book enthusiastically encourages that." Mary R. Mercado, RN

You can get free information about osteoporosis prevention, bone density testing and reports at: **www.avoidboneloss.com**

176 pages, 6" X 9", US $15.95 Available at major bookstores and on the Internet

Order Form

TITLE	Price Each	Quantity	Total
Jewelry Handbook	$19.95		
Gemstone Buying Guide	$19.95		
Ruby, Sapphire & Emerald Buying Guide	$19.95		
Pearl Buying Guide	$19.95		
Diamond Handbook	$18.95		
Diamond Ring Buying Guide	$17.95		
Gem & Jewelry Pocket Guide	$11.95		
Osteoporosis Prevention	$15.95		
Book Total			
SALES TAX for California residents only **(book total x $.0825)**			
SHIPPING: USA: first book $3.00, each additional copy $1.50 Canada & Mexico - airmail: first book $8.00, ea. addl. $5.00 All other foreign countries - airmail: first book $11.00, ea. addl. $8.00			
TOTAL AMOUNT with tax (if applicable) and shipping (Pay foreign orders with an international money order or a check drawn on a U.S. bank.) **TOTAL**			

Available at major book stores or by mail

Mail check or money order in U.S. funds

To: International Jewelry Publications
P.O. Box 13384
Los Angeles, CA 90013-0384 USA

Ship to:	
Name_____	
Address_____	
City_____ State or Province_____	
Postal or Zip Code_____ Country _____	